STUART MCHARDY is a writer, occasional broadcaster, and storyteller. Having been actively involved in many aspects of Scottish culture throughout his adult life – music, poetry, language, history, folklore – he has been resident in Edinburgh for over a quarter of a century. Although he has held some illustrious positions including Director of the Scots Language Resource Centre in Perth and President of the Pictish Arts Society, McHardy is probably proudest of having been a member of the Vigil for a Scottish Parliament. Often to be found in the bookshops, libraries and tea-rooms of Edinburgh, he lives near the city centre with the lovely (and ever-tolerant) Sandra and they have one son, Roderick.

Scotland's Future Culture

STUART McHARDY

Luath Press Limited

EDINBURGH

www.luath.co.uk

First published 2017

ISBN: 978-1-910745-98-4

The author's right to be identified as author of this book under the Copyright, Designs and Patents Act 1988 has been asserted.

The paper used in this book is recyclable. It is made from low chlorine pulps produced in a low energy, low emission manner from renewable forests.

Printed and bound by Bell & Bain Ltd., Glasgow

Typeset in 11 point Sabon by Lapiz

Dedicated to Claire, Roderick and Ishbel McHardy

Contents

Introduction

IN SCOTLAND'S FUTURE HISTORY I drew attention to aspects of our history that are, at the very least, open to re-interpretation. I wrote: 'At the absolute centre of future Scottish history should be one simple idea. That we use what we know of ourselves to find out more'. Following on from that, in this second volume of essays on our past, I have looked at a broader spectrum of ideas. In today's world, at the same time as some societies are becoming psychopathically intolerant, we can also see a growing recognition of people with a variety of different ways of experiencing and seeing the world. The growth of LGBTI groups and advocacy would have been impossible half century ago, even in those countries considered the most liberal. This has happened in large part because of individuals banding together to force governments into facing up to their needs. In turn this has been built on something I mentioned in *Scotland's Future History*: the growth of 'minority' histories, and my contention is that standard political history is inherently flawed in presenting a valid picture of any nation's past.

Scotland, since the founding of Holyrood, has a good record in such areas to date but at a time when the government in the UK is targeting those it should be doing most to help we have to realise that much of what we see as advances in our society are fragile due to the on-going influence of powerful, often multi-national, companies leading to a growing political frustration amongst electorates. Current political systems in much of the world see far too many different sectors of society as problems to be dealt with, rather than constituent parts of an arrangement that is supposedly predicated on working together towards shared aims, or mutual benefit. The chilling Thatcherite phrase 'there is no such thing as society' rings louder by the day and at this time there are growing divergences between what are the constituent parts of a political union primarily due to the resistance against the dominance of one part of that union over the other, particularly as regards Europe.

What has this to do with Scotland's Future Culture? Well we are all defined by who we think we are and that is shaped by our perceptions of what has gone before, not only in terms of political history but in mythology and legend, language, music, dance, story and our own personal genealogies, as well as history in general. Governments seek simple stories to rally people around but that is partly why we are in the situation we are in today in Scotland. The recent explosion of commemorations of the First World War across the media is a case in point. These commemorations were more about the supposedly glorious past of a World Empire than an attempt to come to terms with what was then the greatest slaughter of humans ever perpetrated on the planet. It was as if there was a deliberate attempt to avoid learning any lessons from the blood-soaked debacles of that conflagration.

Governments and political establishments are always very particular about which aspects of the past they want represented. Anything that can be seen as working against their contemporary power is unlikely to be considered, and thus the sacrifice of millions of individuals, and their families, is subsumed in a story about glory and fighting the good fight; a fight in which, as Bob Dylan pointed out, 'We had God on Our Side'. What winner didn't?

The problems of understanding the past are manifold and in SFH I pointed out some of the more blatant distortions of Scotland's past. In this book I am looking beyond the limitations of political history to try and show both how complex, but also how truly inspiring Scotland's past can be.

All history is based on the idea of having a picture of the past that is of value to the present, and the future, and this was true long before literature was invented. I believe we rely far too much on what can be described as grand narratives, or contemporary created realities of the past. This gives a particular view of the past which I suggest leaves out not only a great deal of information which could further our understanding of that past but leads to a somewhat distorted idea of what history is, or, to my way of thinking at least, should be.

In this selection of essays I consider a range of topics from Scotland's past that stretch beyond the normal, narrow definitions of history. It is one of the limitations of modern Western thinking that the specialisation of academics has led to subjects being separated into narrowly defined parameters, which while they may well suit the needs of these specialists and their institutions, can blur any real chance of increasing our understanding of the past. This specialisation sees languages studied not as one of the dynamic and evolving forces of culture and society but as intellectual constructs to be compared and analysed in such depth as almost to make such study irrelevant to all but the specialist. Archaeologists become experts on particular periods, which is of great interest to other similar specialists but what do they learn that will help us understand our pasts better? Much of this is due to processes of intellectual analysis that have arisen as the West developed its Empires, due to overwhelming technical superiority over other peoples, and treated the rest of the planet, and all non-European humanity with little more than contempt. The simplistic application of Darwin's concept of the survival of the fittest to economic matters has given rise to mistaken and pernicious modes of thinking.

When human culture was dependant on oral transmission, the stories of past heroes were probably as important as the myths that were told to explain how the world worked and how we humans should behave in it. While the portrayal of such heroes themselves (of whatever gender) can be seen as similar to the idea of 'Big Men Doing Big Things', the more one studies the great sagas of the past, the more it becomes obvious that the stories reflect the society in which they exist in ways that are radically different from the presentation of history in the modern world, which, rather than arising from within the shared experiences of communities (as oral tradition had, and does yet) is presented from a centralised, and essentially elitist viewpoint.

How we see the world is dependent on what we are told and literary history, generally in the form of the grand narrative, has replaced the oral transmission of stories, myths and legends that were integral to earlier societies and cultures. This book is predicated on the idea that most academically acceptable history is essentially establishment oriented and, as such, can be understood as having a strong propagandistic role in helping to preserve the power structures of today's world. This underlying and often entirely unconscious process is, in British terms (though not uniquely so), tied up with pathological attitudes towards class such as were seen in the recent sycophantic outpourings of media-drivel concerning the Duke of Edinburgh 'retiring' from his royal role at the age of 90.

However, there is, I suggest, a warning we should perhaps tak tent o, as can be appropriately illustrated in the case of the corpus of tales associated with the figure of Arthur. Under the influence of the invading Normans of the 11th century, the focus of this collection of traditional tales that formed a core part of the culture of all of the P-Celtic speaking peoples of this island and Brittany, the hero Arthur became 'King' Arthur. And therein lies the nub of a major problem. Modern history is all too concerned with the actions of so-called elites. In archaeology this translates into the rather unfortunate fascination with the behaviour of what too many scholars perceive as being those at the top of society. I have written of this before and do not wish to go over the same ground but it must be said that, apart from consigning the ancestors of the vast majority of human beings to irrelevance, this approach creates other problems. At a time when the utter venality of those who have their hands on the reigns of power in the British state is daily more evident, we need to realise that one of the ways that elite history distorts our understanding of the past is precisely through narrowing its focus not just in to the 'Big Men', but into political history itself.

What happened in the political arena is given precedence over all other aspects of human society, and behaviour. While this suits the elites of contemporary society and those happy to live in their shadow, it limits our understanding of what happened in earlier times. As humans, we are defined by our cultures as much as anything. In the modern world this has perhaps too often led to a concentration on specific languages, which are one aspect of culture but not its defining core, even if language is of major importance. Not so important however as what language carries. For it is through story, song and poetry as well as music and art that people gain an understanding of who they are and what their culture is – from whence, and whom, they have come.

In this regard, much of what has been presented as important in Scotland's past has, like aspects of history that appeared in the previous volume, *Scotland's Future History*, been subjected to obfuscation, manipulation and in some cases patronising and ignorant distortion. In this present volume, a variety of topics are considered, some of which are definitely outwith political history.

In Chapter One, Going Forward Looking Back, I suggest that we need to approach Scotland's history through analysing the shared experiences of the population at large over time, focussing on the dominant socio-economic patterns that can be discerned as opposed to concentrating on what supposed 'élites' were up to. This leads into the next chapter, Fermtoun and Clachan, noting that the Clearances, Lowland then Highland, removed a pattern of occupation, common across the entire country, that had apparently changed little over many millennia. My contention is that the fundamental importance of the continuity of community underlies all of Scottish culture. In the following chapter, Another Story, I give a brief resume of a lifetime's research into one particular motif that occurs in traditional tales, early histories and in the landscape. This is the theme of the Nine Maidens, tales which were not just common across the Celto-Germanic world but were known across the planet and may well have originally emanated from Africa. This underlines the reality that the peoples of Scotland have never inhabited an isolated backwater but were always part of world culture on many levels.

The following chapter is on Geomythography, which presents a new approach to considering our common past. This approach has developed over many years, following through on research into the Nine Maidens which led to considering how the pre-Christian peoples of Scotland saw their world, and how some of their ideas and evidence of their activities have survived. Chapter Five takes a brief look at the problem of how standard political history has almost totally ignored the role of women in the development of human culture and history. Though things have been changing in this regard over the past few decades, much remains to be done to offset how this has distorted our understanding of humanity's development. I then consider the Kailyard, a term used to define a genre of 19th and early 20th century Scottish literature that has become a byword for what is presented as a couthy, backward and essentially overly twee version of Scotland and the Scots. Though I will be looking only at one story – Ian McLaren's 'The Posty' – I am here suggesting that Kailyard is a valuable part of our culture and that we should celebrate it, not shrink from it.

Following this is an essay about how the Christian Church has shaped so much of what we consider to be Scotland's history. The main focus of this chapter is on the figure of Columba and how his portrayal as 'the dove of the church' is simply propaganda. Saying this is not to make a value judgement on those who gave us our early history – merely to note that a devotion to religion is not the best grounding for developing a balanced view of the past. And as Bob Dylan showed in his song 'With God on Our Side', such attitudes are not unique to the religious.

This leads into a chapter looking at the roles of both story and history in representing, not just the past, but their role in developing how we see ourselves in the modern world. Story has been around for as long as humans have had language, while literature, no matter its current dominance in human society, is a relatively recent development in the growth of our species. This is of some relevance given we now know stories can survive for tens of millennia and, potentially in the case of the stories of the Nine Maidens, for much longer than that. By the time humans left Africa, there is no doubt they were carrying their stories with them.

In Chapter Nine I return to a theme from Scotland's Future History, the Radical agitation in Scotland in the 1790s. While recently there has been welcome attention paid to the Radical lawyer Thomas Muir, and the group known as the Scottish Political Martyrs, the reality is that the demand for radical democratic reform was widespread in Scotland at the time and there were many dynamic and fascinating characters involved.

In the final chapter I look at the remarkable Douglas Young, a man of great intellect and tenacity who was jailed during World War II for his devotion to the cause of Scotland's independence. Included in this is a brief look at the idea of Scotland's sovereignty, which though many people nowadays think is somewhat arcane, I believe to be central to the campaign for taking back our national independence

Underpinning the ideas here presented is the need to try and gain a clear comprehension of just how the culture and community of Scotland have developed through history. Until just a couple of hundred years ago the vast majority, indeed almost the entire population, lived in small scattered self-sufficient communities. In the Lowlands these are generally known as fermtouns and in the Highlands as clachans (see Chapter Three), although technically the Highland versions should be called bailies, with 'clachan' generally referring to such communities that had 'stones', or churches. Many, if not most, of such churches were structures raised on ground that was sacred long before the Christian monks arrived. The idea of this approach is to understand societies that existed in the past through understanding that there was a remarkable degree of continuity within such communities. Many of the fermtouns and clachans that disappeared in the 'improvements' of the 18th and 19th centuries are likely to have been in existence on or around the same locations since at least the Bronze Age, and possibly much longer. Factor in that such communities were almost universally linked through kinship ties, surviving in the Highlands as part of the clan system till the middle of the 18th century, and it would appear that for most people the community they inhabited was central to their lives in ways that have not yet been studied enough.

If a community had survived over millennia, there seems no reason to doubt that the members of that group would have developed specific sophisticated methodologies for dealing with their environment, on both the physical and social level. The idea that they would always need someone to tell them what to do is frankly insulting. Even today in Scotland, crofters, when there is need for communal activity, will come together without the need for some 'superior' individual to tell them what is clearly needs doing. How much more would this have been the norm when everyone lived in the fermtouns and clachans? Yes, in times of war, and in instances of inter-clan raiding, there would be need for leadership. Likewise if boats, or birlinns, were being used, the need for someone to be designated as 'in charge' is clearly necessary. And given that people were inter-related in their small communities, it would only be sensible if the best man for the job was given the role. Once that activity was over, however, why would the person who had control over that activity be seen by his relatives as anything special?

One way of looking at history as it is presented is summed up in the Latin phrase *cui bono* – who benefits. By telling us that the past was always dominated by elites, history plays up the idea that contemporary elites are as natural to human society as breath is to the human body. This is nonsense, designed to keep such contemporary elites in positions of control, and is, as the current state of the world physically, socially and economically suggests, not a very bright idea at all.

Going Forward Looking Back

TO SUGGEST, AS I am doing, that history as it has developed is not fit for purpose (my contention being that the focus on 'Big Men doing Big Things' does not give a true reflection of humanity's past, whether here in Scotland or anywhere else), means it is only right that alternative suggestions should be made as to how we should approach the past. I am not suggesting we throw out all history to date, no matter how tempting that may be to some, particularly to those groups who claim to be driven by religious motives. Rather, in future, I think we have to look across a broader spectrum of both available resources and human experiences to create a better understanding of how our species has lived, and hopefully will continue to live, on this fragile planet. The current fascination with genealogy shows that history is appreciated at a personal level across a wide spectrum, as well as being still part of the establishment education system, and it is such personal interest that underlies what I believe is a viable way forward in attempting a better understanding of our past.

Standard political history ignores the activities of the vast majority of human beings; they are deemed unimportant and irrelevant. This is part of the process by which the increasingly concentrated super-rich of the planet maintain their position. In order to help combat this one of the things we need is different ways of seeing, and I suggest that Scotland's history itself provides the blueprint for such an approach. I have stated repeatedly that the communitarian aspects of Scottish society long predate the fundamentally elitist interpretations of Marx and Engels, and I believe that by focussing on how such ideas of communitarianism survived over remarkable periods of time we can begin to build an improved approach to history. For most of the human occupation of this part of the world, certainly since the last Ice Age as far as we can tell, the vast majority of people have lived in what are nowadays generally referred to as fermtouns and clachans, small kin-related groups of rarely as much as a hundred people, scattered across the landscape and closely related with other such communities.

Such population patterns underlie the social aggregates we see in our history as tribes and clans, and continued to be the norm until the seventeenth and eighteenth centuries for a great many of our predecessors, Highland and Lowland. The pattern can be clearly seen in General Roy's military maps of 1745-6[1]. Their ancestors worked communally to create the great sacred landscapes of Orkney, Calanais, Kilmartin and elsewhere and left traces of how they perceived their own environment across the land, traces of which can be seen today.[2] The point of this is that we can now see that the old elitist notions of how the great monuments were created – some important individual, or perhaps a kingly or priestly class bossing the rest of an essentially subjugated population about – is not the *only* possible interpretation and appears to be one that has been designed to represent humanity in effect as being 'programmed' to be led by those among them who call themselves 'their betters'. Disagreeing with this does not negate the idea of specialists being involved, either in the creation of monuments, or in ritual behaviour; I merely point out that such folk do not need to have had power over others. What the history of the Scottish clans suggests, echoing tribal experience across the world, is that while there were definite differences in status within the clans, even the chiefs could be removed if their activities were seen as detrimental to the interests of the community as a whole. And there lies the key: *the community as a whole*. Think of communities as organisms and it makes sense that over time they will develop processes that work for the benefit of everyone. Even if some folk are better off or have more status than others (situations that do not necessarily coincide) no one is left behind.

This was the antithesis of feudalism, but in the present it is potentially much more than that: it is a model for future thinking that is rooted in the idea of the sovereignty of the people. In the modern world it is becoming ever clearer just how governments have been suborned by the rich, whether it is the USA (with Great Britain ever in close attendance) permanently fighting small-scale wars which are extremely profitable for the arms industry, as is the maintenance of the military structure itself (a point made in January 1961 by President Eisenhower in his famous 'farewell speech'[3]), or the governments of China and post-communist Russia being run by brutal oligarchies whose sole aim seems to be to join the ranks of the super-rich. War, after all, is the best of all capitalist exports, with shells and bullets requiring constant replacement for so long as it (war) continues. It does not have to be this way, despite what the mainstream media say.

In the story of the human species over time, the role of the tribe has been central. When the Roman historian, Dio Cassius, in 217 referred to the tribes of Scotland, he said of them:

> Their form of rule is democratic for the most part, and they are fond of plundering; consequently they choose their boldest men as rulers.

He didn't mean that they had an electoral system with universal suffrage, but he meant something. It may well be that he understood that the tribe came first and that any chief's role was seen as an organic part of such a society and not deemed to be set 'over' it. This idea of the community may never have been spelt out, but it appears to be intrinsic to the functioning of tribalism. After all, the entire fabric of such societies rests on the notion that every individual within the tribe is related to every other, even in cases where it wasn't technically correct. By belonging to the tribe, or clan, you were part of a community that claimed descent from a common ancestor, or ancestors.

A weel-kennt Highland story, common to many clans, tells of a smith willingly sending his seven sons into battle one after the other to defend their chief, all of whom fell, after which the smith himself strides forward to his death. There is no way this could have actually happened unless they all subscribed to the notion that the chief's importance was for the clan, their community as a whole, and thus that he was more important than any of them, or even all of them. The key word here is willingly; this would not happen if the chief were merely an overlord or master, as people are not that stupid. The story may well be apocryphal; stories after all do have to have a point, and the point here would be to underline that precise concept of loyalty – loyalty to the clan, not to the individual who happened to be the chief at that particular time. Within all such tribal systems the chiefs are part of the community not their overlords.

I believe that it is this essential aspect of tribalism that underpins the thinking behind the 1320 Declaration, in which the assembled signatories, speaking on behalf of the 'whole community of the realm of Scotland', say of King Robert: 'if he should give up what he has begun, seeking to make us or our kingdom subject to the King of England or the English, we should exert ourselves at once to drive him out as our enemy and a subverter of his own right and ours, and make some other man who was well able to defend us our King'. This is rooted in the fundamental idea of community and one of the reasons historians have been so keen to condemn tribalism as 'primitive' may well be because most tribes are societies in which the community defines for itself what is best, and not just the would-be bosses.

My contention is that if we build our history on an understanding of how communities actually functioned in the past rather than concentrating on the actions of those who have been presented as their leaders, and thus the most important people, we will begin to understand ourselves better, and perhaps begin to be able to plan for a better future for our children and grand-children. The insanity of current economic thinking where it can be seriously proposed, for example, that fracking in the Central Belt and the gasification of coal beneath the River forth are viable future developments shows how out of kilter the lust for wealth is with the actual physical world and our interdependence with it. The push for fracking in Scotland is not predicated on any community benefit arising from the energy produced, despite slick PR blandishments telling us 'we' need this energy: rather it is to make money. You cannot breathe, drink or eat money.

The idea of looking at basic communities in the past arose partly from work I have been doing in developing the idea of Geomythography. This process approaches the modern landscape through an awareness that human society is continuous and that the continuities of culture that shape each individual society can to some extent be understood through their effects on their landscape over time. In the Highlands of Scotland, the existence of museums such as the Highland Museum at Newtonmore, that are essentially the remains of old communities,[4] show us that the population of those parts lived lightly on the land. They were not rich materially, but from what we know of both Gaelic and Scots culture (much of it surviving both from before the introduction of literacy, and parallel to it) they were culturally rich. They also had healthy if hard lives, and one small fact illustrates that the modern historians' Hobbesian representation of our past as being always fraught with horror till the development of the modern centralized nation state is itself a construct. Again Dio Cassius, in 217, mentioned a food that was gathered and kept by the inhabitants of Scotland:

> ...and for all emergencies they prepare a certain kind of food, the eating of a small portion of which, the size of a bean, prevents them from feeling either hunger or thirst...[5]

This same food is attested in later clan times and is the earth pea, also known as the kale pea, the tuber of a plant called the

Bitter Vetch. Its life-sustaining properties have been researched and are as remarkable as that suggested by Dio Cassius.[5] Now, it may seem of no more than passing interest that people in Scotland over a millennium and a half apart were using the same standby plant. It is also undeniable that the benefits of this particular plant were known across most of Europe for a very long time. However what this does underline is the reality that the fermtoun and clachan existence of the people was remarkably conservative. Things would only change when they had to, or when there was obvious advantage in changing. This tendency can account for the numerous occasions when people were prosecuted by their local Presbyteries for indulging in what were seen as essentially 'pagan' practices, particularly in the sixteenth and seventeenth centuries. Such practices had been useful in the past, or had been understood as being helpful, so why shouldn't they work today? This conservatism is perhaps also why many of the healing charms used by witches and others incorporate Christian terminology and even belief; a kind of eminently practical belt-and-braces approach, again rooted in local experience.

In the modern world where capitalism is constantly promoting change – ever newer, faster, fancier mobile phones is a contemporary example – the idea that one should hold onto what served your ancestors well might appear odd. For most of the human existence on this planet it has been the norm. As we live at a time when the current dominant socio-economic system serves its masters by exporting war, destroying habitats and looting natural resources, the ways of our ancestors have a certain attraction, no? And I suggest that this is just as true of how we should approach history.

History, like story before it, has the purpose of providing a credible, coherent vision of society to which its members can subscribe. At the moment, this 'vision' supposedly requires all of us to follow the elitist narrative that has arisen over the past few millennia, driven by a combination of urbanisation, literacy, centralization and increasingly rampant greed. If instead of focusing on the past deeds of sociopathic and often psychopathic 'leaders', we actually were to look at the continuities of life for communities as a whole we would see a different picture. Elitist history plays up war and schism and downplays peace and continuity. We can change that. Elitist history constantly reminds people that they are of no importance compared to 'their betters'. We can change that.

Scotland is not unique in having been subjected to this process. It is however unique in that all societies, as all individuals, are unique. And it is our very uniqueness that unites us; no two snowflakes are the same, nor are any two humans. Back in the '60s and '70s many of my friends were aghast that I could call myself a nationalist, even if the term I used then, and now, is cultural nationalist. How could I? The same friends would regularly sign petitions and send letters of support to different indigenous peoples across the globe supporting their fight against encroaching capitalist and imperialist powers. Their cultures were precious, yet I was supposed to subsume the support of my culture into some supposed international movement that united us along class lines. Strangely enough it was always the 'working classes' of England (rather than Ireland, France or Germany) I was urged to align with. I demurred then, and still do. I am a Scot. I love my country's history, culture and landscape, and (mostly) its people. I spend a great deal of time on land that was effectively stolen from its original inhabitants by a venal crew of uncultured buffoons under royal direction, but it is still my country, and if this and my attachment to the stories, songs, art and music of my country makes some people consider me a 'blood and soil' nationalist, that is perfectly fine by me. Those that use such language are in the main thirled to the perpetuation of an Establishment that exists to serve the interests of an ever-concentrating class of pirates who believe the entire planet and its inhabitants are there to be pillaged for their personal benefit. Their opinion is of no matter to me, even if the lickspittle mass media of Britain constantly trumpet their whinings.

1. http://maps.nls.uk/geo/explore/
2. See Chapter 4 Geomythography
3. Military-Industrial Complex Speech, Dwight D. Eisenhower, 1961 http://coursesa.matrix.msu.edu/~hst306/documents/indust.html
4. http://www.scotlandsbestbandbs.co.uk/en/museums-in-the-highlands-and-isle-of-skye_50098/
5. http://www.loebclassics.com/view/dio_cassius-roman_history/1914/pb_LCL177.265.xml?readMode=recto
6. http://www.thesouthernreporter.co.uk/lifestyle-leisure/outdoors/ancient-soutra-hospital-findings-updated-1-2875031.

Fermtoun and Clachan

'[...] what we are witnessing along the Fen-edge in the Neolithic period is growth and continuity, not the disruption that would have attended the rise to power of a vigorous new leader [...] communal organization and motivation remained essentially bottom-up; held together by local tribal or family ties and obligations [...] I can see no evidence whatsoever for any supra-local authority, any Big Man'[1]

I HAVE LONG been drawing attention to the problems of 'Big Man' history both in lectures and in various writings, and it is a sign of the changing times in archaeology when someone as notable as Professor Pryor, of 'Time-Team' fame, takes a clear stand against one of the tenets of Big Man history. His particular interest is in the Stone Age in the Fens of England. Things are somewhat different in Scotland. In *Scotland's Future History* I mentioned the existence of similar occupation patterns in the Highlands and Lowlands. In the Lowlands these communities were known into recent history as fermtouns, and in the Highlands, while the more accurate name is bailie, they have come to be known as clachans. A clachan is actually a bailie with a church, but the phrase 'fermtouns and clachan' has come to have a particular Scottish resonance.

This description dates from 1973:

Certain of the rather similar settlement forms of Atlantic Europe, including the Scottish clachan, may have their origins in prehistory. The clachan, or fermtoun, consisted of a small hamlet of people engaged in joint farming, run-rig agriculture; the term clachan is of Highland origin [and means a baile with a kirk] that of fermtoun of Lowland derivation. Neither of these forms of settlement remains in their original state, except in ruined footings in some of the Highland glens, as a result of the sheep clearances in the 18th and 19th centuries, and occasionally in a very modified form, as hamlets of smallholdings between tracts cleared for new, improved farmlands in the 18th century in fertile parts of the Lowlands.[2]

Scholars have noted that many such small settlements survive in the modern landscape as place-names, one in particular *kirkton*, deriving from *kirktoun*, a place where a church had been erected. These are often at crossroads, reflecting the fact that the congregations of these churches were spread out across the landscape. However, due to the physical effects of 'improved' agriculture, many such names cannot be claimed with any certitude to be on the sites of such an earlier settlement, except in those cases where the church itself survives. As noted, the Gaelic place-name *clachan* – literally 'stones' – often indicates a former kirktoun, and this is due to the fact that probably the only stone buildings across most of the Scottish medieval landscape were churches. A few such places, like Fowlis, in south-west Angus, which still has its twelfth century church, retain something of these earlier settlement patterns.

A great deal is known about the specific agricultural practices of the run-rig system that these communities used. They all had in-bye land, intensively manured and farmed strips of land where crops were grown, and an area of out-bye for pasture and rough-grazing. Beyond that was forest – a term which initially meant unfarmed, or, more properly, uncultivated, land which provided a range of materials which were of great importance: wood, berries, healing plants, and wild animals which were hunted. There is a confusion that arises from thinking that farming only consists only of enclosed field farming. I suggest that even nomadic peoples regularly visiting certain locales to avail themselves of specific food resources can be seen as using a form of farming. An example of this can be seen in the indigenous Australian use of fire to stimulate vegetation growth, reflecting an interaction with their environment that appears to have been relatively common amongst nomadic people. Very few communities have actually been 'primitive', a pejorative term that shows just how elitist too much history has become. The term run-rig refers to the fact that the land was divided up in strips and such strips were re-allocated annually so there was a fair sharing of resources throughout the community. This allocation process was not only an economic necessity but, like many of the activities of such communities, was one in which everyone participated. The problem that we face in considering the importance of this way of life is that most commentators to date have focused on the specific practicalities of economic life in these communities and have ignored their wider historical and sociological relevance. Pryor hits the nail smack on the head when he tells us that such communities were 'held together by local tribal or family ties and obligations'.

The myth of modern progress that underpins so much of modern Imperialist history relies on us believing that tribal societies were 'primitive' and 'backward-looking' institutions whose relevance to humanity has long gone. As Pryor points out our ancestors lived in societies that were defined and dominated by such ties and it is an undisputable historical fact that such ties continued to play a significant role in Scottish society into at least the middle of the eighteenth century. And it is true to say that in certain sectors of contemporary society, kinship is still a defining parameter at various 'levels'. In England the pattern had begun to change at least as early as when the country was taken over by the Romans and the imperial socio-economic structure imposed. Later feudalisation by the Norman invaders followed by enclosures and other 'improving' practices has meant that there were few, if any, remnants of this pattern of basic social structure left there into modern times. On the other hand it was the continued existence of this type of socio-economic structure that allowed Bonnie Prince Charlie to raise an army in the Highlands in 1745 in a fraction of the time that would have been necessary to raise a contemporary standard national army.

For the term clan is simply a Gaelic word for 'children', the children of a common ancestor who had founded the tribe. Whether there was actually such a common ancestor matters less than the reality that the ties that bound these societies together relied on believing that he had existed. The idea that tribal existence is essentially primitive is one that has predominated in history for several centuries but there are strong reasons for re-considering how we perceive tribal structures, particularly in Scotland.

The tribe as a form of social and political organisation appears to go back to the Stone Age and when we reflect that even in Scottish terms that means that it was in existence for thousands of years, this should give us pause for thought. In parts of Scotland this means that the tribal system possibly functioned for at least seven thousand years. Before considering what this has to tell us about our history and our contemporary landscape it should be noted that the fermtouns of the Lowlands did not disappear till the 'improvement' of the 18th and 19th centuries. Like their cousins in the Highlands, the occupants of these places lived on the lands of their ancestors and it is not pushing matters too far to suggest that in some cases that may well have meant their family had been on the same area of land for millennia. As far as we know, over the five to seven thousand years previous to the Lowland and Highland clearances, there had been no great displacement of population in Scotland as a result of invasion. The various invaders over the years – Romans, Vikings, Northumbrians and English – have either been repulsed or absorbed. So, such continuity is extremely likely to have been the norm with the immediate family group functioning as part of a larger social aggregation. We know that inter-clan raiding was the norm in the Highlands from at least the Iron Age to the eighteenth century, by which time the same behaviour had disappeared in the Borders (but only since the early seventeenth century). And for most of its existence when the Scottish Parliament referred to clans, this included the kin-groups of the Borders. It was only in the nineteenth century that clan became used of Highland society alone. This has been exacerbated by much of the scholarship associated with the Gaelic revival, and while understandable, it is regrettable in that it plays into the British government's well developed policy of divide and rule.

The main form of obvious wealth in both Highlands and Lowlands was cattle. In both areas people raised cattle and grew crops and were at a fundamental level economically self-sufficient. While the larger tribe could, and often did hold, stores of food under the control of the chief as a standby against crop failure, or human-induced disasters, the primary function of each fermtoun and clachan was to keep its people fed. Throughout human history raiding has been an integral part of cattle-rearing tribal societies. Cattle were moveable so could be 'lifted'. Whether this 'lifting' was the cause of the rise of warrior societies or the role of warriors preceded such raiding matters little. The reality is that such pastoral societies as they are known, have warrior tribes at their very core, and raiding was an absolutely central aspect of male behaviour. This was not considered theft, but an exercise in skill and bravery which, given that in northern latitudes the raiding took place between harvest and the onset of winter, meant more food (if successful) for the community over the winter: a win-win situation, if not for the victims of such raids. To defend one's community against such raiding or to pursue the raiders to regain stolen cattle, it helped to have a social organisation that meant you could call on support from nearby settlements. The actual process of such cattle-raiding, developed over millennia, had its own set of rules and was never the simplistic theft that centralising authorities, first in Edinburgh then subsequently in London, liked to portray it as. Inter-community raiding has been part of pastoral, cattle-rearing societies over much of the globe for a very long time and was still in existence till very recently in some parts of Africa.

It seems worth asking: how late were the Lowland clachans united in tribal structures akin to those of the Highland clans? We know of the strong family ties in the Borders: the Nixons, Kerrs, Scotts and Douglases to name but a few. Their loyalty to their kin is well known and, even if the population of the Lowland areas of Scotland had become more peaceable by the mid-seventeenth century, it is worth reflecting on the reality that in earlier times their socio-economic structure was very like that of their cousins to the north.

It is clear that when the Romans arrived they were met by tribal warriors – they tell us this – and at the putative battle of Mons Graupius, in the leader of the Caledonians (as they called the Picts in the first century) we have a man leading a confederation of tribes who is not said to have any particular status and is certainly not presented as a king or any kind of aristocrat.[3] Such confederations of diverse tribes still existed into the 18th century with the Siol Alpin, the Clan Chattan, and the very diverse Clan Donald. While, from at least the time of David I in the thirteenth century, centralizing power in Scotland was attempting to pull the teeth of the armed societies that the clans represented, there was enough vigour left in this ancient way of life to provide the backbone for the Jacobite risings of the eighteenth century that came perilously close to succeeding in restoring the Stewart dynasty, and may well have done so if the Scottish Jacobite Army had not retreated from Derby in 1746. And it appears, most of the actual members of the Jacobite Army in 1745 would have apparently been happy to have a new Stewart king, for Scotland.

The fermtoun and clachan system was much more than a system for training and supplying warriors. The cattle-raiding which provided the vast majority of the military activity among the clans for millennia was a seasonal activity. Only after the harvest was in and enough supplies laid down to survive the coming winter would the men embark on raiding. At this point I would like to make it clear that I believe the idea that there was an elite class of warriors in every clan who provided the cateran or cattle-raiders flies directly in the face of the evidence. If only an elite were trained warriors then why did General Wade estimate the potential number of Highland warriors in the mid-1720s as twenty two thousand? To provide such numbers of elite warriors would mean that there wasn't a hillside in Scotland that wasn't intensively farmed to support a population sufficient to support such elites in turn. Not everyone was the same in clan society and not everyone had access to a full set of arms, but the men all could, and would if necessary, fight. The weapons used by some of the Highland troops at the Battle of Prestonpans in 1745 were scythe blades on poles, a cheap and easy substitute for the traditional and expensive Lochaber axe, and they were devastating against both men and horses. The need for such weapons shows that there were many Highlanders who could not afford to have the classic set of arms. Yes, there were elite warriors. The men who provided the chief with his bodyguard had special status in the clan and may well have been composed mainly of his close kin, but all men – and, I suspect, a few women as well down the ages – were trained as warriors. As young men, the chosen heirs of the Chiefs would have to lead a raid to show their mettle but it is notable that the vast majority of clans had a *capitan*, or captain, who was the military leader.

The pattern of fermtouns and clachans existing into the eighteenth century can be clearly seen on General Roy's military maps of 1745-6.[4] These not only show the scattering of small communities in both the Highlands and Lowlands but also have the new 'improved' estates of the time, generally in remarkable detail. The maps provide a snapshot of an ancient pattern of existence about to disappear forever. Another aspect of the Roy map's depiction of this pattern of occupations is that its illustration of the continuity of such land-usage from very early to the dawn of the modern age shows to what extent

Scotland was actually feudalised. Very little. It is also important to realise that we can approach trying to understand our past by concentrating on land-*usage* and not land-*holding*. For much of our history the idea of land-ownership, if it had any meaning at all would have been understood to the majority of the population as community land-holding. The awarding of land charters from the time of David I was part of the centralising process of government structures and would have meant nothing to the majority of the population. It is tempting to think that, up to at least the thirteenth century, much of the Lowland areas of Scotland could have been managed under the same ownership pattern as that of the Highlands. This was essentially based on the concept of *a glaibh* – by the sword – by which the chiefs saw their communally held lands as being ensured and established by the fact that anyone trying to take over the clan lands would be resisted – by the sword. The effects of the charters handed out by successive kings of Scots meant that eventually chiefs grew to realise that they had a legal right to the lands they and their kin inhabited. They could, and so did, take personal possession of what had been the land of the community as a whole. This insidious land-grab was part of the centralizing process of spreading the King's law over the entire country. Previously the holding of the land in common was based on custom and practice but, as we have seen, that was custom and practice with a very long history indeed, possibly thousands of years. The breaking of this bond with the land, of course, broke the ties between the clan and the chiefs and it is actually offensive to see many of these modern lairds strutting around pretending to be clan chiefs when their ancestors' actions destroyed the socio-economic basis of the clans they claim to lead – for personal gain. The process has been presented almost universally as part of 'progress' – an idea that effectively means that the rich get richer and the rest get screwed.

There is much more to the *clachan and fermtoun* system than just its capacity to support a military force that could be ready to march off to battle in a few hours, even if it is important to realise that, except when called upon to resist invaders, the Highland warrior was trained for battle not war. The inter-relationships of the people who lived in this way over millennia meant that their social system had the time to develop sophisticated means of ensuring its own survival. This is where Professor Pryor's observations can be seen to have particular resonance. At the time of Roy's maps the vast majority of villages and small towns that dot Scotland's countryside had not yet come into existence and the small scattered collections of houses that comprised the clachans and fermtouns covered the country.

In the Highlands the change from the head of a clan being the chief of a community claiming a shared ancestry and working communally to a landowner set on milking the maximum personal financial gain from the land that he and his kin had worked for millennia is well laid out in Dodgson's *From Chief to Landlord*, though I reckon he underestimates the cynicism and moral vacuity of such people.

If, as I believe, the clan system of the Middle Ages is a direct development of earlier times, in that the tribal structure had been the bedrock of society for potentially millennia, then the experience of such communities suggests a sophisticated inter-relationship with not just the environment but also with the very idea of community itself. There are weel-kennt instances of chiefs being removed from their positions for various reasons, all of which can be summed up as them being unfit for the job in the eyes of the clan, or tribe or community. It seems that such practices would have been the norm in all the tribal areas of Scotland which, up to the end of the First Millennium, means most of it. And, as Roy's maps show, the pattern does not seem to have changed much even by the middle of the eighteenth century. This was not long ago. Given the continuity of occupation patterns and what we might call the historical community experience that culture derives from, we have a particular potential for understanding our past in Scotland that is not common elsewhere. The survival of the fermtouns and clachans means that despite the agricultural activities of the past three centuries there are still potentially many sites throughout Scotland that would bear further investigation. For these communities were the inheritors of the knowledge of their own past and how they related to the environment, and, in terms of land use, astronomical alignment and sites of sacrality, there is much we can learn. Our current capitalist society is only a few centuries old and though the inhabitants of the fermtouns and clachans in the seventeenth and eighteenth centuries may not have been materially well off, particularly by modern standards (for some), they were the inheritors of a long culture that was rooted in the landscape they inhabited, and possessed sophisticated levels of knowledge of their environment beyond our ken.

As an example of such cultural sophistication I want to finish this piece with a particular example.

In the south and east of Scotland, where the P-Celtic languages were spoken, the tales of Arthur were common. In the best known of these tales Arthur goes off on a pilgrimage to Rome at which point his wife Guinevere takes up with his nephew Modred. This leads to a battle in which Modred and Arthur are killed, though in some variants Arthur is taken off to the Isle of Avalon by Morgan and her eight sisters (see Chapter 8). Behind this apparent tale of Royal lust and treachery there is a simple moral tale. In the fermtouns and clachans of the distant past, where every man was trained as a warrior, sleeping with the wrong person could be disastrous. People would stand by their own kin when disputes arose and in cases of adultery it is easy to imagine how not only an individual community but those around it, where the protagonists in such disputes had relatives, would become involved. It is, at a fundamental level, a tale of a taboo against adultery. The same reality probably underlies the story of Diarmuid's betrayal of Finn McCoul by fleeing with Finn's wife Grainne. In passing, it should be noted that though the Arthurian material, by the time it became literature, was concerned with 'aristocratic' and 'royal' personages, it all arose from tribal societies where there were chiefs rather than kings in any modern sense of the word. And chiefs in tribal societies are part of that society, not looking down from above, despite the adolescent fantasies of Big Man history

Human psychology is pretty constant and we can be sure that there were cases where people were attracted to the wrong person. This is where the sophistication comes in. It is well documented that even into medieval times the great feasts where the people gathered were wild affairs. As the nineteenth century folklorist James Frazer says of festivities like Beltain, Lammas etc., 'we may assume with a high degree of probability that the profligacy which notoriously attended these ceremonies was at one time not an accidental excess, but an essential part of the rites.'[5] And an essential part of the rites which may well have had a cathartic effect for both individuals and communities. Burns, in 'The Holy Fair', describing a massive countryside meeting purportedly to hear rival preachers deliver sermons, put it another way:

> There's some are fou o love divine
> An some are fou o brandy
> An mony jobs that day begin
> May end in houghmagandie
> Some ither day.

1. Pryor, Francis, *Home* Penguin London p 121
2. Milkman, R N1973 *The Making of the Scottish Landscape* London P 82
3. Tacitus (Ed Mattingly) 1970 *Agricola and Germania* Penguin London 30. p 79
4. http://maps.nls.uk/geo/explore/sidebyside.cfm#zoom=9&lat=56.2302&lon=-3.1424&layers=3&right=BingHyb
5. Frazer, J 1994 *The Golden Bough* UP Oxford p98

Another Story

I HAVE MENTIONED on several occasions the importance of the Ness of Brodgar in recalibrating Scotland's past. The idea that Scotland was on the fringes of human society, awaiting enlightenment from the south, is simply not tenable any more, no matter how much the idea suits the British Establishment and their hangers-on. There are other potentially even older links with the rest of the world which are, at the same time, more tenuous but run very deep. In his *Life of Merlin*,[1] Geoffrey of Monmouth, who gave the world 'King' Arthur, draws upon a truly ancient motif when he has Arthur taken off to the Isle of Avalon after the fateful Battle of Camlaan, by Morgan and her eight sisters. Much has been written of the potential historicity of Arthur, and several authors, myself included, have noted that the supposed twelve battles of Arthur which so many scholars have tried to identify, can all be given reasonably solid Scottish locales.[2] This is also true of Camlaan which, it has been reasonably suggested, is Camelon near Falkirk. Important tales derived from myth and legend find their own locales and one is not necessarily the origin of all others. If there was an historic Arthur, as opposed to a heroic figure amongst the P-Celtic speaking peoples (Britons of Strathclyde, Bretons, Gododdin, Picts, Welsh) much like Finn McCoul amongst the Q-Celtic speakers (Irish, Scots Gaelic, Manx), the most popular Scottish candidate amongst contemporary scholars is Artur MacAedan, son of the King of Dalriada, said to have died in 596 in a battle with the Miathi or Maetae, a tribe I suggest lived south of the Forth-Clyde line. Be that as it may, the story Geoffrey gives us has the island of Avalon being inhabited by Morgan and her eight sisters who, he tells us, were known for healing, prophecy and shape-shifting. This sounds very much like any similar group of priestesses from many parts of the pre-Christian world and there are a range of references to them in story, place-names and church dedications across Scotland.[3]

They crop up as a group of saints, as the companions of other saints, had several wells dedicated to them and have at least two stories that tie them to Pictish Symbol Stones. I first came across them in a story attached to Martins' Stane, north of Dundee, which has them being killed by a dragon. They are also linked with the ancient figure of the Cailleach, the Hag of Winter, and to Bride, Goddess of Summer, the pair of whom in one sense can be seen as aspects of the same supernatural being, a type of Mother Goddess, associated with fertility, weather-working and landscape creation. Stories of these groups are linked to such diverse locales as Ben Nevis, Abernethy, and Priory Island in Loch Tay.

Their association with Avalon, in the personages of Morgan and her sisters has a particular potential locale in the east. All stories in pre-literate times were set in the known landscape of the communities that told the stories – how else would they be relevant to children whose education relied on story – and given suggestions that Camelon near Falkirk was the site of the final Arthurian battle of Camlaan, the island in the Forth that best fits with the idea of Avalon is the Isle of May. May in Scots means 'maiden', and archaeology has shown that this was an important site in both pre-Christian and early Christian times. Other areas would have had their own version of Avalon but it is worth taking note of the fact that several nineteenth century writers compared the nine maidens of Avalon with a similar group of nine women on the Isle du Sein off the north coast of Brittany, known in modern times as the Island of the Druidesses. They too were known for healing and prophecy.

There is another group of nine women who crop up in Arthurian material, the nine witches of Caer Lyow who, in the story of Peredur[4], give him his weapons – the hero being given his final training and/or his weapons by a woman, or a group of women, is a recurrent motif in many traditions – before he turns on them and slays them. There are also several Nine Maidens stone circles in different parts of England and, as we shall see, the possibility of a link lasting across millennia is not only possible but appears to be distinctly probable. The nine maidens crop up in a few instances in Ireland and are widely known in Norse mythology. The idea that there was no contact between the peoples of Scotland and Scandinavia before the arrival of Viking raiders is clearly nonsensical; there has been cultural contact between Scotland and Scandinavia for millennia. The obsession with all things 'Celtic', partly because of the erroneous notion of the Scots originating in Ireland, has blinded generations of scholars to the reality that Scotland has long been part of what can be seen as a Celto-Germanic cultural world. The truth is that defining any people by the language they speak is not a particularly helpful idea.

In Norse and Icelandic sources groups of Nine Maidens crop up as witch-like figures, as companions to goddesses, and perhaps most intriguingly as the mothers of the God Heimdal, watcher of Asgard. They also crop up in an ancient text, linked with a great World-Mill which effectively was said to have created the physical world. One reference from a ninth century Hebridean Norseman called Snaebjorn also mentions a whirlpool. Given that one Welsh source mentions nine maidens as tending the cauldron of the goddess Cerridwen, which some scholars suggest is the Corryvreckan whirlpool, the world's third largest, between Jura and Scarba, we are in swirling waters indeed.

The on-going obfuscation of Scotland's history does seem to have started a long time ago and the question has to be asked: why is the world's third-largest whirlpool not better known in Scotland? That its existence has deliberately been suppressed appears quite likely when one takes note of the fact that the standard gazetteer of the nineteenth century Scotland, *Groome's Ordnance Gazetteer of Scotland*, claims that this phenomenal geo-physical event was named after 'a tidal race in the Aran islands' off Ireland's north coast. This is clearly non-sensical and such suppression suggests that the importance of the Corryvreckan in pre-Christian thought was considerable. What is strange in this regard is that the whirlpool is mentioned in Adomnan's Life of Columba where Columba is said to have stopped the dangerous whirlpool by throwing earth he had blessed into it.

There are stories linking the whirlpool with the Cailleach which are clearly mythological and may be very old indeed. Whether there were Scottish equivalents of the island 'Druidess-es' of Brittany is as yet moot, even if Geoffrey of Monmouth's story of Avalon suggests it is possible, but if there were then it would not be beyond the bounds of possibility that such a group were based near the whirlpool. The Gulf of Corryvreckan is just off the coast of Argyll opposite Kilmartin, the site of a truly mag-nificent sacred landscape from pre-Christian times. Till relatively recently the whirlpool was still known amongst local fishing communities as 'the breath of the goddess under the waves'.

However the Nine Maidens are not just restricted to north-west Europe. Some commentators have suggested they were inspired by the idea of the Greek Muses, following that tired old trope of influence always coming to Scotland from the south. The idea all European civilization started in the Medi-terranean area is hardly tenable in light of the Ness of Brodgar dig. Investigation of the Muses shows there to have been sev-eral groups of similar priestess-like groups in Greece, most of whom were, like many of the Scottish ones, linked specifically to mountains and/or sacred wells, and known for healing and prophecy. Other instances of similar groups exist in French tra-dition and recent work in Portugal has uncovered several more, though most refer to early saints. These are likely to have been based on earlier pre-Christian groups in a similar fashion to the

Pictish Nine Maidens. In Catalonia there is another group of them which is of quite a different order.

In a Magdalenian cave-painting at El Cogul, near Lerida in Catalonia there is a group of nine females dancing round a spectacularly priapic male. Time and again when we come across the Nine Maidens in different times and places, they are linked to a single male – the Nine Maidens at Strathmartine are linked with Martin, whose name is attached to the Symbol Stone, Arthur and the maidens of Avalon, Heimdal and his nine mothers - and this fifteen thousand year-old painting shows that the idea predates the retreat of the Ice Age in our part of the world and the arrival of the first humans. The nine also survived into twentieth century Siberian shamanistic belief as the nine daughters of the God Solboni with whom, in some localised traditions the aspirant shaman had to sleep. This too happens in other stories concerning the nine and is reminiscent of the idea of Heimdal having nine mothers. Some of the tales refer to the nine living on an island and there is a well known motif in traditions from across the globe of Islands of Women – the Irish Gaelic Voyage of Bran has the hero and his seventeen companions landing on just such an island where each finds a companion – 2X9? Here again we see the absorption of earlier ideas into Christian tales, in a similar fashion to the Christian policy of building their churches on ground already sanctified by long years of local ritual. Re the Siberian survival of the nine into modern times, a previously unknown version of the Voyage of Bran was collected in Perthshire not very long ago, for, despite the almost tyrannous power of literacy, stories, and the ideas underpinning them, do sometimes survive. Tales can survive even major cultural change including the replacement of language. The stories of King Arthur that have gone around the world in English were originally told in Old Welsh and other ancient P-Celtic dialects, and the same can be said of the Q-Celtic stories of Finn McCoul and the Fianna.

In the stories of the Nine Maidens we can see this process quite clearly and there are traces of the same idea in many parts of the world including China, Japan and even the South Seas. Nine is of course is a universal magic number and again in very diverse cultures the necessity of repeating an action nine times, or things happening nine times, constantly recurs.

The idea of the Cailleach and the Carlin seems to go back a very long time indeed but it seems the motif of the Nine Maidens may be of equal antiquity. Both of these motifs survived in many locales in Scotland – so can we say that the old ideas lasted longer or remained more deeply rooted here than in most of the rest of the British Isles? I think perhaps we can, precisely because our history is different. We did not have the English experience of being part of the Roman Empire, nor, despite constant repetition of the idea, did we ever have any real Norman feudalisation and our experience of Christianity was different from Ireland's because of the Reformation.

Presbytery Records from the Reformation and after show just how persistent 'pagan' practices were in Scotland. We are who we are, just as other nations and societies are who they are. This is not about being better than anyone, merely recognising that our history and culture are distinctive and much less influenced by external sources than we have been led to believe by our current education system. The influence that Scotland has had on the growth of the modern world is well known. Arthur Herman's book, *How Scotland Invented the Modern World*, shows it quite clearly. But there is much about our past that remains unknown and part of this is directly because we have been fed so much disinformation. I was accused in a review of my last book of being a 'wha's like us' type of historian, the clear sub-text being that I was overly-nationalistic and incapable of critical thought. Well I am happy to be a 'wha's like us' type of historian because I believe that Scottish culture is not only distinctive and unique but that my native land has had a powerful influence on other nations and peoples over many years. I want that recognised and it is sad to say that still today too many Scots are quite happy to recognise that oppressed peoples around the world have the right to hear their own stories while pretending that all is well here. It isn't.

The safe and essentially bourgeois attitude of many historians whose primary concern is all too often to protect their careers and to never rock the boat, is not what is needed if we are to let the future generations of Scottish children fulfil their potential as human beings. They have a right to know their own history and also to gain a better perspective on Scotland's place in the world. It was through studying the Nine Maidens that I became aware of just how much of our history has been ignored or suppressed, primarily because it didn't fit in with the safe bourgeois Establishment propaganda that has passed as our history for too long, but the search has taught me other things. It is often claimed that people are more 'socialist' in Scotland than elsewhere in the British Isles (a.k.a. England) and many of the arguments against nationalism to which I have been subjected over the decades run along the lines of the need to be a true internationalist and not a narrow-minded *Scottish* nationalist. The need was to stand by our 'brothers' in the rest of the UK (not our brothers in Spain or France or Germany, strangely enough). Well, the communitarian underpinnings of Scottish society long predate the elitist analysis of Marx and Engels – 1320 anyone? – and the idea that any specific political philosophy can solve everyone's problems is, given human diversity, a tad far-fetched. Also, this argument would never be put to a Native American, an Inuit, a Maori, an African Bushmen or any number of indigenous South Americans. I think that to be a proper inter-nationalist I have to be a nationalist first and that is precisely how I can truly appreciate the rights and traditions of people of other lands and societies, not by pretending that there is some overweening political philosophy that negates the glorious diversity of our human culture, including Scotland's. That way a homogenous and stultifying globalisation lies. So here is an international perspective.

Probably the oldest version of the Nine Maidens I have come across hails from Kenya. It is the founding myth of the Gikuyu people and it involves nine sisters, their father and as in so many cases, a sacred mountain, in this case Kilimanjaro. Remembering that the Great Rift Valley, where the earliest humans have been traced, runs through Kenya, do we see in this ancient tale a story that first came out of Africa as humans began to spread across the globe? It seems at least possible that it did. And if so, over the immense time since that spread began, the story has taken root in different cultures and flowered. We may never know for sure but this is certain: I only know about the potential origin of this apparently important aspect of human culture down the millennia because I was interested in my own, my native culture.

1. Parry, JJ 1925 *Vita Merlini* University of Illinois Press p16
2. McHardy SA 2001 *The Quest for Arthur* Luath Press Edinburgh
3. McHardy SA 2003 *The Quest for the Nine Maidens* Luath Press Edinburgh CH 1, 2

Geomythography

Geomythography is the interpretation of specific locales in the landscape, generally originally pre-historic through a combination of oral tradition, place-names, landscape analysis and archaeology. The process is a means of finding new perspectives and interpretations to hopefully further the understanding of earlier stages of society.

THE PROCESS OF Geomythography is rooted in the awareness that the passing on of tradition in pre-literate societies is predicated on certain continuing realities. In many cases, such as Scotland, communities have survived within the same environment over remarkable periods of time. This has created a rootedness, not just in terms of physical environment but in socio-psychological terms, that have led to considerable depths of continuity between the generations. This can perhaps be understood as an on-going cultural relationship with the physical environment, and the stories set in that environment, which exists simultaneously at an individual and communal level. One way of understanding this is to see 'ancestor worship' not as something inherently religious but much more akin to respect, respect for those who paved the way for contemporary society, physically – by handing on prepared ground with the knowledge of how to use it, much as understanding of how to read the weather was passed on – and significantly, in the field of human inter-relatedness with that environment. The respect for the ancestors in traditional societies is accompanied by a sense of responsibility towards coming generations who are expected to perpetuate the continuity of the community. In pre-literate societies the mode of transmission of such cultural values is oral tradition. This can be understood as not only referring to traditional stories but also specific data such as site-specific weather lore and place names. While many place-names are essentially topographical, ie. descriptive of the landscape, others have mythological or ritual connotations (see Appendix B).

We must also remember that humans are animals and that the rootedness of such communities is matched by the rootedness of individuals within such communities and the physical environment. This in turn created an attachment to the land that was essentially visceral rather than intellectual. What is known as Diaspora poetry and song underlines this reality in many cultures.

In *Building The Great Stone Circles of the North,* Colin Richards makes the following point when writing about folklore associated with ancient monuments:

> ...objects become invested with meaning through the social interactions they are caught up in. These meanings change and are renegotiated through the life of an object [...] those things are always in the process of becoming; in this sense we can say, monuments are always in the making through discourse.[1]

This is particularly relevant in those societies and locales where the population remains essentially localised over long periods of time, as appears to have been the situation in most of pre-eighteenth century Scotland. People lived on the land inhabited by their ancestors. Within the clan system, which arose directly from earlier forms of tribal society, local beliefs may well have been handed down over truly remarkable lengths of time. It has been established in Australia that some of the traditional stories of the aboriginal population may well have originated over thirty thousand years ago.[2] The dates of some of the flint scatter from Elsrickle at 12000 BCE[3] suggest the possibility that some of the localised material in Scottish folklore tradition may well have considerable antiquity. Some underlying ideas, such as that of existence being in some way based on an understanding of feminine fertility, are likely even older, perhaps having already been part of our culture when humans first arrived here.

What is of considerable import is that, as Richards points out, 'the monuments are in the making'; and effectively they have been for a long time. This can only have helped to reinforce important locales within contemporary culture time and again. So places associated with supernatural figures like the Paps – breast-shaped hills (below) – have become the focus of a range of sociological and communal activities and, as they are still prominent in the landscape, their everyday cultural relevance continued till very recently, and even arguably to the present day. Appendix A shows the variety of constructs that can be, and have been associated with some of these sites, going far beyond the out-dated notion that everything on the top of a hill must have been a military structure.

There is also a level of practicality that can be discerned in much of what is considered to be mythological thinking. How was the land created? Where did humans come from? Who controls the weather? These are fundamental questions for all human societies and in many early mythological constructs we can see that the explanations of such deep questions are based on a practical approach to the environment and how to survive in it. It is a fundamental tenet of the geomythographic approach that we retain an awareness of both practicality and continuity in dealing with early human society. It is also of considerable importance to note that so many supernatural figures, mythological, legendary and religious are clearly derived from human prototypes.

In *The Pagan Symbols of the Picts* (2013, Luath Press, Edinburgh, *passim*) I presented an interpretation of the symbols based on the concept of an underlying worldview that life itself was driven by a force that was essentially feminine. This idea was specifically based round interpretation of material relating to those sites known in Scotland as Paps. These breast shaped hills, perhaps deliberately echoed in localised ritual mounds, are the locales of what I have referred to as 'clusters' (see Appendices A and B). These clusters include a considerable range of different examples of human interaction with these specific locales and include: the breast shapes themselves, perhaps perceived of as deliberately shaped by the Goddess figure associated with landscape creation; the stories of powerful female (and sometimes male) figures associated with the locales; ancient monuments suggestive of ritualised behaviour; place-names referring to mythological and legendary figures and ritual behaviour; oral traditions referring to weather patterns linked to the role of the powerful female figures as weather-workers.

What is clear is that these Pap sites conform to the ideas suggested by Professor Richard Bradley where he suggests that significant locales stand out from the landscape because of 'their striking topography'.[4] It has also become clear (see *Carlin Maggie* below) that some sites seem to have been the foci of a further level of interaction where specific viewpoints of the site bring extra levels of interpretation. Just as the Paps themselves were the focus of belief through stories of the powerful supernatural beings associated with them, so it seems they had extra layers of meaning when seen from specific locales. The extent of how much this is interlinked with solar and lunar alignments – as appears to be the case with the Carlin Maggie site – is something that merits further investigation.

The process arose initially from analysing traditional oral material associated with specific sites of antiquity, often ancient monuments.[5] Over time a pattern emerged where it was clear that specific shapes (initially Paps) were repeatedly associated with certain supernatural figures. Most dramatically these were the Cailleach in Gaelic-speaking areas and the Carlin in Scots-speaking areas, which I have written about extensively elsewhere. The activities of these figures in landscape-shaping, weather working and their association with significant geophysical realities and events in the landscape e.g. Ben Nevis, the

Corryvreckan Whirlpool, North Berwick Law, etc., illustrates the depths of their rootedness in communal belief. What became apparent was that certain sites and locales had become not just significant in themselves but had attracted cultural aggregations that speak of their importance over time. The repeated association of mountain top sites with supernatural females is particularly obvious. It is also apparent that many such places were the sites of rituals. Echoes of such ritual behaviour can be seen in place names like Lomond, deriving from the P-Celtic *llumon*, a beacon or chimney,[6] and Craigshannoch on Bennachie possibly deriving from the Scots *shannack*, Halloween fires.[7] Similarly there are a number of 'Bel' names across the country which appear to refer to the activities associated with Beltain. Through understanding that such sites and locales were the foci of ritual and belief, it became clear that further interpretation is possible. I have discussed this elsewhere but am now in the position of giving this process of inter-disciplinary interpretation itself the name of Geomythography and as an illustration of how the process can be productive I include here recent discoveries made in the physical landscape of Scotland.

Uamh nan Deargan, Scarba

I have been visiting the island of Scarba for several years with a study group that focuses on the Corryvreckan and its role in mythology, tradition and literature. The name *Uamh nan Deargan* translates as Cave of the little Red One and I visited it for the first time in 2009 because in the tale of *Mac Iain Direach* in Campbell's *Popular Tales*,[8] collected circa 1860, the action, while supposedly set on Jura, actually starts at *Creagan nan Deargan*, the rock of the little red one, which is on Scarba. This anomaly intrigued me and consulting the os map (Pathfinder No 365) I noticed there was a cave there. The tale is full of interesting mythological material, some of it linked directly to the Paps of Jura, which are themselves of some significance in pre-Christian thought. The story also includes references to the Seven Big Women of Jura who in some respects conform to the model of Nine Maidens. Coming toward *Baigh* (bay) *nan Deargan* you walk through a natural stone arch in the outcrop known as *Creagan nan Deargan* and are immediately below the entrance to a cave.

The cave is not far from the opening of the Gulf of Corryvreckan, between Scarba and Jura, which contains the world's third biggest whirlpool and is associated with the Cailleach, a supernatural female figure, who tradition suggests was originally a goddess figure. A major fault line which cuts across the entire island runs through the roof of the cave and its name, *Uamh nan Deargan*, the Cave of the Little Red One, may be related to the fact that the northern side of the cave is composed of red-streaked rock. The fact that the floor of the cave is flat and smooth is clear indication of human activity here, and

Stone arch looking north east

initial investigation suggests this was at least as far back as the Neolithic. The evidence of human occupation is confirmed by scorch marks from a long-term hearth fire on the northern wall.

Within the cave itself is a naturally-occurring outcrop of stone closely resembling an upside-down human skull. It is approximately the right size for a new-born baby and is in the cleft of rock that forms the cave itself. The cave's name, the upside-down skull shape, and the red-streaked rock combined, lead to the speculative possibility of this having been some sort of birthing site. Its proximity to the Corryvreckan and its association with a goddess figure perhaps reinforce this, especially as the Cailleach in some surviving tales is clearly presented as a dual figure whose other half is Bride, the Goddess of Summer, and a striking symbol of fertility and rebirth. Bradley's ideas regarding the archaeology of natural places would suggest this is a site that would have evoked strong reactions in the early occupants.

Cave

Skull

Lochnagar

In the summer of 2011 I went to Lochnagar with my son Roderick. The intention was to visit Meikle Pap. The name Lochnagar was given to the mountain in the nineteenth century supposedly to avoid embarrassing Queen Victoria (for whom Prince Albert purchased the Balmoral estate in 1852) by using its earlier name *Beann na Ciochan*, the hill of the paps or breasts, there being Little Pap, south of Meikle Pap. This is of course similar to the name of Bennachie, which is likewise named for its prominent nipple shaped peak, nowadays known as Mither Tap, but earlier as Mither Pap. This underlines the association with the Cailleach/Carlin, the landscape-shaping and weather-working supernatural female of both Gaelic and Scots tradition. She is commemorated on the Lochnagar massif by the place-names *Caisteal na Caillich* – another lesser peak of the massif - and *Allt na Cailleach* the stream which runs northwards along Glen

Muick. The name Glen Muick may also have some significance, as I have pointed out elsewhere,[9] that there were strong traditional associations between early Goddess figures and porcine animals in different societies. Another nearby place name is *Coire na Ciche*, the Corrie of the Pap, and further north on the massif above the river Don there is *Creag nam Ban*, The Rock of the Women, which may denote a site of fertility rituals, as are associated with similar named places elsewhere.

Sadly there are no extant tales regarding the Cailleach relating to Lochnagar but this may well be due to the fact that the surrounding glens were cleared of their indigenous populations to make way for the shooting estates set up in the nineteenth century. On reaching the top of Meikle Pap I was struck by the odd shapes of the rocks which, like Carlin Maggie and other significant hill-top sites, are composed of dolorite. Dolorite takes on smooth and fascinating shapes over time, very often appearing to

Lochnagar 'eyes'

be carrying aspects of the human form. On the topmost rock of the summit there are two holes which look like eyes. Such holes were thought in previous times to have happened naturally, but this seems unlikely. It may also be relevant that in many cultures the eye is seen as a specific symbol of goddess figures.[10] Whether there is any link between the concept of Lochnagar as sacred site and the annual Midsummer Solstice pilgrimage is unclear and I can find no references to the event before the 20th century. At the least these 'eyes' present what Bradley refers to as 'striking topography', though if they are man-made, or enhanced, their location on the summit of Meikle Pap is remarkable.

Cnoc Brannan

In the summer of 2013 I was on the summit of Ben Ledi, part of the summit of which is called *Cnoc a' Cailleach* and where there are reports of Beltane fire ceremonies as late as the nineteenth century. I noticed what appeared to be an unusually evenly-shaped hill to the east in Glenartney. Such symmetry hints at human involvement and, on consulting the map, I discovered this was *Cnoc Brannan*. Brannan is potentially a variant of Brendan or Bran, both of which names have a significance in early Christian and pre-Christian materials from Scotland, Ireland and Wales. The Welsh connection to Bran is particularly interesting because of the shared linguistic/cultural heritage of the Welsh and Southern Scottish P-Celtic speaking tribes (and probably Pictish tribes to the north) of the 1st Millennium. It is possible that the Q-Celtic derived Brandan variants are rooted, like so much early Christian material from these islands, in earlier constructs. I researched the area further, finding that the stream to the west of *Cnoc Brannan* was *Allt na Caillich* and that there had been a couple of cup-marked rocks found in the area. I then went to Glenartney and walked up the burn. I found the following site just a couple of hundred metres from the bridge. It appears to be an unrecorded disturbed chambered cairn.

It was through the combination of landscape reading, place name analysis and an awareness of the depths of tradition associated with this particular name that I noticed the *Allt na Caillich* and, by following that up, made the discovery of the unrecorded chambered cairn. This is a precise example of how the process I refer to as geomythography can be of use in archaeology.

Carlin Maggie

On the side of Bishop Hill overlooking Loch Leven in Fife there is a dolorite stack or pillar called Carlin Maggie. A local tale recounts how Maggie was the leader of the witches who regularly gathered in the Lomond Hills and she became so sure of her own powers that she ended up fighting the Devil himself. As in all such tales there could only be one conclusion and it is said that Maggie, coming off worse in the struggle, ran off and was turned into this stone pillar by a blast from Auld Hornie. The Lomond Hills are known as the Paps of Fife and like other similar places are clearly associated with pre-Christian ritual belief and, in all likelihood, ritual activities (above and Appendix A). The Carlin in Scots tradition is a match for the Cailleach in Gaelic tradition and there is sufficient evidence to suggest that surviving folklore attached to them denotes them having been goddess figures in pre-Christian times.[11] In 2014 I decided to visit the stack, which is on a very steep part of Bishop Hill in an area that has been extensively scarred by quarrying. All photographs I had seen of Carlin Maggie to that point had been taken from the south and showed a somewhat phallic pillar of

rock. I approached from the south west and headed north past the stack. It was then that I noticed something quite remarkable about this particular dolorite pillar. Viewed from the west, it has a shape that is strikingly redolent of the well-known 'Venus' figures from Malta and elsewhere. This further underlines the potential association with an early goddess figure here, and further research has shown there is more to be investigated in the landscape of the Lomond Hills, Loch Leven and the Ochil Hills to the west.

On a subsequent visit to a potential 'natural site' a few miles east in the Ochil Hills,[9] further aspects of the Carlin Maggie site were noticed and these figure in 'MYTHOGRAM1' which exists as a digital story on YouTube.[12] Further such digital pieces are planned focussing on the island of Scarba and Ballachulish.

Appendix A Cluster sites
Bennachie
Initially Beinn a Cioch, the hill of the nipple or pap.
Craigshannoch, Rock of the Samhain Fire
Maiden Stane
Maiden Causeway
Mither Tap
Stone circles at Chapel of Garioch, Chapel o Sink, East Aquhorthies and Hatton of Ardoyne.
Standing stones at Hatton of Ardoyne, Monymusk and Tombeg
Symbol Stones at Logie
Whitecross
Whitewell

Lochnagar
initially Beinn a Ciochan, the Hill or Mountain of the Breasts
Alltcailleach Forest
Caisteal na Caillich
Carn an t-Sagairt Beg and Mor. Cairns of the Priest

Cnapan Nathraichean, The Knoll of the Adders (Bride or Druidic reference?)
Coire na Ciche, Corrie of the Nipple or Pap
Glen and Loch Muick, from Muc, a pig or swine
Little Pap
Meikle Pap
White Mounth

Paps of Fife

East and West Lomond Hill. Lomond means beacon
Maiden Bower – geophysical feature used in fertility rite
Maiden Castle – not a fortification
The Carlin and her daughter – geophysical feature: Carlin is Scots for Cailleach
Devil's Burdens – geophysical feature
Early church site at nearby Orwell
Earthwork in Glen Vale
Early Christian Symbol Stone with fish and cross on W. Lomond Hill
Fort on East Lomond Hill
Scotlandwell and its priory
White Craigs

Paps of Jura

Jura is originally Norse and means Deer Isle
The Paps are three mountains one of which is Beinn Shantaidh, the Holy Mountain.
One of the others Beinn an Oir, has Sgriobh na Caillich where a hag is said to have slid down the side of the mountain.
This location is also associated with the Seven Big Women of Jura, who in tradition had the Glaibh Soluis, the Sword of Light. They may have originally been 9 in number (see McHardy 2003).
Jura is probably the site of the Columban Hinba.
The Corryvreckan at the north end of the island has many Goddess associations and traditions and is one of the world's

seven significant whirlpools. Its spiral shapes, thrown into the Atlantic Tide are known as the Breath of the Goddess under the Waves and may have inspired northern European use of the spiral motif.

On the east of the island at Small Isles Bay there are Rubha (point) na Caillich and Rubha Bhride and Eilean Bhride.

Paps of Lothian
Used to describe North Berwick Law and Arthur's Seat
North Berwick Law is a major landmark and linked to 17th century witch activity.
Arthur's Seat has wells, hill-forts (?), a chapel and an ancient fertility site, the Sliddery Stanes.

Appendix B Cluster elements
Significant elements in locating potential Goddess sites. It is suggested the significance of these elements increases with frequency and proximity.

Wells – particular noteworthy dedications are Saints Brendan and Bride, and potentially Ninewells but wells are significant in themselves.

Antiquities – most hilltop sites are given as forts but their significance as Beltane/Samhain fire sites may be more significant; likewise earthworks of various kinds and cairns can be of significance, particularly if associated with specific names – eg. Shennach, a variant on Shannach, the Scots for Halloween fire. Stone circles are always a sign of a sacred site whereas without other supporting evidence it is impossible to be so definite about single standing stones.

Early church sites – particularly when on mounds – virtually proof of a previous site of sanctity.

Dens – many dens are associated with early saints, witches, supposed serpent worship. Their continuance as places of local activity can be construed as an example of social continuity.

Landmarks – instances like figures in the natural landscape or particular shaped hills reminiscent of the female body often have a place name element referring to this significance – or have associated ideas/tales in local history and folklore.

Islands – in both lochs and sea islands, probably because of being surrounded by water – water is the stuff of life and this can be seen as the virtual blood of the Goddess, underlining the importance of wells.

Appendix C

White/Fin – white is traditionally seen as the colour of sanctity.

Nevay/Navay/Navie – as a separate word or word ending this refers back to nemeton – a sacred grove. Can be difficult to spot as in Slocknavata in Galloway.

Bride/Bridget/Breedie – can be first or last element. A Mother Goddess, symbol of fruitfulness and regeneration, specifically associated with Summer and independently existing in England, Ireland and Scotland.

Cailleach/Cally – in many forms.

Ban – particularly as in *nam ban*, of women.

Cioch – nipple.

Dun – generally assumed to mean fort but see above.

Law – often distinctively-shaped and standing alone, many laws have folklore associations or distinctive names, suggesting they have a meaning beyond 'hill'.

Mam – breast

Nathrach – meaning the adder.

Pap – there are quite a few of these, often with 'clusters' around e.g. Mither Tap on Bennachie

Seat/Suidhe – again these names tend to have specific significance.

Witch/Witches – significant if associated with other elements.

White in place names occurs frequently near ancient sacred sites throughout the UK

Note. At Bennachie there is the name Bruntwood Tap, and at the back of Fannyhill, near Muckhart, we have Burnt Wood.

This could be a reference to the burning of ceremonial fires at Samhain and Beltane, as Lomond surely is.

Notes.

1. Richards, C 2013 *Building The Great Stone Circles of the North* Windgather Press Oxford p292

2. Isaacs, J 1980 *40,000 Years of Australian Dreaming* Lansdowne Press Willoughby NSW

3. http://www.biggararchaeology.org.uk/pdf_reports/ MESOLITHIC_REPORT 2010.pdf.

4. Bradley, R 2000 *The Archaeology of the Natural Places* Routledge N.Y. p6

5. McHardy, S.A. 2003 *The Quest for the Nine Maidens;* 2005 *On the Trail of Scotland's myths and legends,* Chapter 2 ; 2012 *The Pagan Symbols of the Picts,* Chapter 7. Luath Press Edinburgh

6. Watson, W.J1986 (repr) *The Celtic Place-names of Scotland* Birlinn *Edinburgh p 212*

7. *The Concise Scots Dictionary* 1985 Aberdeen University Press p 605

8. Campbell JF (1994 reprint) *Popular Tales of the West Highlands* V2 p93

9. *The Pagan Symbols of the Picts* passim

10. Crawford,O.G.S. 1958 *The Eye Goddess,* MacMillan NY

11. https://en.wikipedia.org/wiki/**Cailleach**

12. https://www.youtube.com/watch?v=Ls1HGq3XkF4

The Cutty Stool or The Distaff Side

THE POINT HAS been regularly made that in general women feature little in history, other than when they are filling in for a man. Thankfully this is something that is changing and in terms of Scotland's history. In books such as *Damn' Rebel Bitches*,[1] in which Maggie Craig shines a welcome light on Jacobite women from a still under-researched period of our history, we can see that change. However, the general point remains that women are deemed surplus to most history. This has quite remarkable ramifications for our understanding of the past and I want here to point out something that it is totally speculative. One of the supposed defining developments of the 'civilisation' of human-ity is the creation of pottery. This was a major technological advance in the Stone Age and made the storage and transporta-tion of food and liquid much easier. On thinking about this over a considerable time I began to consider that the original cre-ation of pottery – and like most human developments it would have happened at different times in different places – must have been made by women. Why? Women tended the hearth fires of communities. Modern ideas of equality tend to brush over the reality that throughout most human societies there has often been clear differentiation between what has been deemed men's and women's work. And tending the hearth fires, while looking after the youngest children of the community, has always been mainly women's work. Men would light fires when they were off hunting, or working at a distance from the home, and they would use such fires for both cooking and heating.

However, the fires that women tended were permanent. The tradition of smooring or smothering fires overnight that lasted well into historic times in Scotland ensured that the hearth or home fire never actually went out. That this practicality of always having fire to hand also developed more ritual overtones cannot be denied, but at the heart of each home within the small communities of Scotland's fermtouns and clachans there was fire tended by women. Women were also the ones who cooked most, as they had to feed the children, so their need for storage of both ingredients and cooked food would be greater than that of men. Given also that women had a greater need for washing clothes than men – babies and small children always require some sort of bathing – it seems more than possible that it would have been women who noticed that certain types of mud along watersides had a tendency to harden in the heat of the sun. That combined with their knowledge of fire makes it worth considering whether it was women who first developed pottery.

Men would soon see the advantage of pottery but would still have less use for it than women. Women had opportunity, need and knowledge. Most importantly they had that experience of constantly working with fire. This is unprovable. But if women did manufacture the first pottery, then there is a question that follows from it. Was it also women who became the first metallurgists? The same arguments apply and I would go so far as to say the idea of Bride as the goddess of Fire in pre-Christian north-western Europe may well reflect this. Could this have been what was behind the development of the tradition of the sisters of Bride at Kildare tending the perpetual sacred fire?[2] If this was indeed the case then it seems quite possible that the first metal objects were tools rather than weapons, an idea that may even be testable. Why? Not because women are inherently less argumentative than men but simply because the needs of the food supply and the preparation they were involved in could have driven such technological development. From the development of cutting blades for food gathering and preparation it is not too big a step to see that men would have quickly seen the benefit of developing hunting implements. And we should perhaps remember that hunting too has generally been a communal activity, even when it degenerated into sport for kings and other social aberrations. The point here is that by critiquing standard history we open up new ways of understanding the past, ways that can maybe help us gain a clearer picture of humanity's past.

Most history courses that I teach begin with that simple point: women generally only figure in history when they are doing a man's job. Such weel-kennt figures as Mary, Queen of Scots, Elizabeth I of England or Catherine the Great of Russia only feature because there was no man available for that job at that time. It is a bizarre way of looking at our past that fifty per cent of all human beings who have lived are considered surplus to the needs of history. This of course is because history has been controlled by elites for so long, and elites are at this point in time dominated by men, often supposedly 'aristocratic' and undoubtedly rich, and getting richer at our expense. Things have changed in the past half century with the growth of women's and so-called minority history (what are elites if not minorities?) and we are at last beginning to see that the story of humanity is not just a glorified parade of posh-boys. There are a few women who feature in Scotland's history who are not from the so-called upper strata of society. One of them shows up in the popular tale of the Protestant Reformation in Scotland being started when Jenny Geddes threw her stool at the minister in St Giles Kirk after he began reading from the new Common Prayer Book. One of the reasons it rings true is that the Edinburgh Mob who flourished in the seventeenth and eighteenth centuries, often in specifically political fashion, consisted of both men and women. In later times, too, the role of women in the protests against Highland clearances in the nineteenth century is well attested.

The women of Glasgow, led by Mrs Mary Barbour during WWI saw off the blatant rack-renting of the propertied classes while their men were off fighting for Empire and Freedom, or suffering wage cuts to further enhance the inflated profits of the shipbuilders and arms manufacturers. The illicit whisky-making of the seventeenth and eighteenth centuries involved as many women as men. And we should perhaps remember that in the small communities that held most of our population for so long, the defined roles of men and women developed over time to meet the needs of the community as a whole.

I have written elsewhere of the role that story can play in helping to enhance our understanding of the past. Winners write the histories but the losers still talk to each other, and it is not in the hands of the Establishment to determine what finds a place in our on-going culture, no matter how hard they try. Songs and stories preserve attitudes and ideas that can open our eyes to alternative interpretations. This of course is a complicated process and just as I would advise everyone to take a critical approach to all written history, we must take the same approach to other source material.

To return to Jenny Geddes, the story goes that on Sunday 23rd July 1637 the minister in St Giles' Kirk on the Royal Mile began to read from the Book of Common Prayer that the King, Charles I, was intent on forcing the use of.

He wanted to re-model the Presbyterian Kirk of Knox and Maxwell into a version of the bishop-led Anglican Church of England. As far as most Presbyterians were concerned this was a step towards re-introducing Catholicism and was a direct affront to their own ideals and beliefs. Presbyterian doctrine was rooted in the fundamentally democratic idea of the congregation being their own masters, choosing their own minister and was underpinned by the idea of universal literacy. The idea seems to have been that everyone should be able to read the Bible, and then there would be no need for an interlocutor between the population at large and their God. There was no need for priests to interpret what you could read for yourself. Not everyone in Scotland was a Presbyterian of course, but the influence of the idea of every parish having its own school providing education to the population at large has had a major effect on how Scotland has developed.

In 1696 the Scottish Parliament passed an 'Act for settling of schools' calling for a locally funded, Church-supervised school to be set up in every parish in Scotland. This commitment to increasing literacy meant that discussions about often trivial aspects of Biblical interpretation became endemic at all levels of Scottish society (see the following chapter on the Kailyard) and no doubt goes a long way to explaining the reputation of the Scots for disputation or, carnaptiousness. An English friend once told me that the definition of a Scotsman was someone who could start a fight in a phone-box, which is reflective of the same thing. Jenny Geddes, if in fact she ever existed, which some people have doubted, appears to have been of the carnaptious kind. She is said to have picked up the three legged cutty stool she sat on – the pews were reserved for the better off in St Giles' in those days – and flung it at the minister shouting 'Daur ye say the Mass in ma lug?'

Immediately, others of the congregation leapt to their feet and began throwing their stools and anything that came to hand, including their Bibles. There was general uproar and things quickly got out of hand. The general population of Edinburgh, the common folk, with no direct say in the governance of town or country, had a long tradition of rioting – the Edinburgh mob was famous throughout Europe until late in the 18th century. Unrest spread throughout the city and it wasn't long before there were other disturbances in towns and villages throughout Scotland as well.

There were negotiations in Edinburgh between the rioters and the Privy Council but matters simply got more heated. The group negotiating on behalf of the protesters were known as the Tables and there was no chance of their demands for a withdrawal of the Anglican liturgy ever getting the agreement of the King. This in turn led to the drawing up of the National

Covenant in 1638, initially signed by a large crowd, both men and women, in Greyfriars Kirkyard on 28th February.[3] Copies were made and circulated throughout the country and it was signed by tens of thousands of people. It was a demand to defend the Presbyterian religion and was in part based on an earlier document of 1581 called the Native Confession, which had been drawn up to resist attempts to re-instate Catholicism in Scotland. It is telling that the Covenant specifically rejected the King's innovations on the grounds that they had not been scrutinised and ratified by the Scottish Parliament and the General Assembly of the Church of Scotland. While this was to a great extent about religion, there is a clear underlying aspect of the democratic will of the people seeking expression. In November the bishops and archbishops were formally expelled from the Presbyterian Church. Now, Charles was a keen believer in the Divine Right of Kings and there was no way he was going to accede to the wishes of the common folk. So he raised an army and the Bishops' War began. This was just the beginning of what has become known as the War of the Three Kingdoms which raged throughout Britain for the next decade until the Parliamentary New Model Army under Oliver Cromwell triumphed over the King's forces and Charles was beheaded in 1649.

In today's Edinburgh you can see exactly how women have been ignored in our history. The town is full of statues, virtually all of them men – Queen Victoria has two, one at the Kirkgate in Leith and the other atop the Royal Scottish Academy in Princes Street. The only other female statue is in Festival Square Lothian Road, and it is an anonymous statue of a woman and child as a monument to the sufferings under apartheid in South Africa. This illustrates that the mind-set that sees women as unimportant has been as strong among politicians as historians. Of course Edinburgh has a reputation, in the rest of Scotland as being a peculiarly Anglicised, conservative and extremely stuffy place (even those off-comers like myself who love the place can hardly deny this perception) but just a few miles down the road there is welcome sign of change.

In Tranent since 1995 there has been a statue of Jackie Crookston,[4] one of a dozen local people shot dead on 29th August 1797 by dragoons following a riot against the Militia Act, which conscripted young men into the British Army. This act, which caused other riots elsewhere, was particularly odious as, in true British style, those with money could pay to have their sons removed from the conscript list. The statue has Jackie Crookston beating a drum, accompanied by a child, and it is regrettable that despite having such good examples like the Clearance Memorial at Golspie to draw upon, the civil government of our capital city have not done anything to redress the imbalance of public art in Edinburgh. This same city is seen by many across the globe not just as an example of art and creativity, but of democracy, following not just the establishment of the Holyrood Parliament but the unfolding of an independence campaign conducted peacefully, and in the main (excepting the London-centric media and their Scottish clones) in a civilized fashion.

1. Craig, M2000 *Damn' Rebel Bitches* Mainstream Edinburgh

2. http://www.kildare.ie/community/easysites/ kildareheritage/?page_id=44

3. http://bcw-project.org/church-and-state/ crisis-in-scotland/scottish-national-covenant

4. https://en.wikipedia.org/wiki/Massacre_of_Tranent

The Kailyard

IN THE MODERN world the idea of history has been changing. It is no longer simply about 'Big Men doing Big Things'. We have seen the growth of Women's History, an upsurge of interest in minority history on many levels, and also, linked to genealogy, an increasing awareness of local history. As yet, though, history is still very much restricted in most people's minds to political history, the doings of nation states and powerful individuals such as kings and emperors. After all, this is what is taught in our schools. The emphasis on using local sources for teaching in the 'Curriculum for Excellence' is a welcome sign of change, a step in the right direction, but I would suggest there is a long journey ahead in terms of teaching Scotland's future generations their nation's and its people's history. I strongly believe that to have a clearer idea of what the past was like we have to be aware of the cultural aspects of society at any given time, and by that I do not mean the government sponsored bourgeois art-forms of opera, the ballet, symphonic music, etc. These art forms have their place in society, but they are only some manifestations of what constitutes cultural activity. In the selection of a canon of what is 'acceptable' or 'proper' art we face the same problems as we do with history: the selection of importance based on the biases of a self-defined elite. The ideas behind such selections are clearly based on the ridiculous notion that has driven so much manipulation of history: that some people are born 'better' than others; richer, more powerful probably, certainly, but 'better'.

The Kailyard School is a term used to describe a particular genre of Scottish fiction writing that arose in the last years of the nineteenth century. The works so designated have been generally disparaged as being overly sentimental and idealized. Mainly set in rural locations, its writers tended to avoid the harsher realities of life and focus on the mundane and domestic. This has led to it being seen as representing an idyllic picture of Scottish life, far removed from reality. However there is no doubt about the popularity of Kailyard, derived from the Scots word for 'cabbage patch'. The use of kail, a specific native form of the cabbage family was ubiquitous in rural Scotland in the nineteenth century and earlier, so much so that term itself in Scots has also become synonymous with soup or even food in general. What cannot be doubted was the great popularity of those writers generally considered to be members of the Kailyard school, principally J.M. Barrie, S.R. Crockett, Ian MacLaren, George MacDonald and Gabriel Setoun.[1] Their popularity spread beyond the boundaries of Scotland, selling well throughout the English speaking world and not solely within the Scottish Diaspora. Criticism has consistently been levelled at the Kailyard for presenting what was essentially a romanticized portrayal of an idealistic past that had never really existed. Its popularity was in no small measure due to the fact that the country was living through turbulent social change brought on by ever increasing industrialization and the decanting of tens of thousands of people from the land into the cities. Nostalgia for a freer, healthier lifestyle is quite understandable.

Often using the short story form, the Kailyard writers were themselves generally from respectable bourgeois backgrounds and their work was accepted very much by the various Presbyterian churches of the time. John Watson, writing under the name of Ian McLaren, was himself a Free Kirk minister. This of course has added to the perception of the Kailyard as being non-threatening and conformist. Many later commentators have gone so far as to suggest that the Kailyard school presented a kitsch vision of Scottish life. Things, however, are not quite that simple. One of the notable facts about many of these authors was their use of the Scots language, particularly in reported speech, reflecting the fact that the majority of people at the time still spoke Scots. This was despite the proscription of its use, along with Gaelic, within the education system in the Education (Scotland) Act 1872. One has to posit the question as to whether those who saw themselves as the defenders of the literary canon have been, if not actually offended by the use of Scots, at least uncomfortable with it. It has long been a cliché in Scottish life that to 'get on' you should speak English rather than Scots. This perhaps did not apply to later commentators such as the poet Hugh MacDiarmid, who loathed the Kailyard 'school', but his attitude towards the Scots language was unashamedly elitist and essentially egotistical. No only did he ken best, he kennt that he kennt best. His promotion of 'Lallans', which was a form of the Scots language but was a deliberately created one, had little to do with the living language of Scots which featured so strongly in the Kailyard. While MacDiarmid was clearly a positive influence, I believe his role has been exaggerated.

There are problems with literature and language that are common across the world. The elite histories of nation states are used in conjunction with the idea of a canon of acceptable literature to suppress not only dialects other than those spoken by the elites but actual separate languages. In the United Kingdom it is not so long ago that those involved in broadcasting almost universally used what was known as Received Pronunciation (RP), a deliberate replication of the strangulated tones of the 'upper crust'. That this is a dialect of English is undeniable but it is only one of many dialects, chosen as a standard by the elite and their supporters throughout education, media, etc. This means that for a long time not only was there suppression of other dialects of English – but also the suppression of other languages. In the UK this has meant active state discrimination against Gaelic, Scots and Welsh as well as the recently-revived Cornish, and, for so long as the whole of Ireland was part of the Empire, Irish.

This is common across the world. In Europe we have France where there are other languages such as Basque, Breton and Occitan; in Spain there is Basque, Catalan and Galician; in Italy, Ladin, Sardinian, Veneto and others. These and more have been subject to varying degrees of proscription or persecution. Such discrimination, I believe, is all too often accompanied by a school of thought that exists in capital cities that I have called metrovincialism. By this I mean the disparaging habit amongst capital city elites to dismiss the rest of their countrymen and countrywomen as 'provincial', that is concerned only with local matters, and thus 'backward', 'off the pace', 'uncool' and 'certainly not up-to-the-minute'. The real problem for many groups in various societies is not so much the insularity of the capital elites but how it is aped by those in other parts of the country who see their own status and power as dependent on the power of the capital elites. This quote is from the American scholar Richard Blaustein:

> ...the Scottish lairds deliberately stripped themselves of Gaelic [and Scots] language and culture in their eagerness to assume metropolitan English values and norms, voluntarily committing ethnocide and linguicide.[2]

This I believe is linked to why we have been given such a skewed idea of the Kailyard writers. Their works were extremely popular in Scotland, England, and throughout the Scottish Diaspora. While there is little doubt that the Kailyard stories often present idealised situations, they also dealt with significant aspects of the human condition. I believe that one of the principal reasons they were disparaged was because most of the reported speech in such works was in Scots. Sir Walter Scott had done the same thing in several of his popular novels, but by the time of the late 19th century the British Empire was in full swing and the pseudo-Anglicisation of certain levels of Scottish society reflected this. The Scots language, like Gaelic, had been effectively proscribed in the 1872 Act and the Gatekeeper mentality was growing in strength. Drawing attention to this type of historical reality in the past has lead to some people suggesting that I was indulging in typical 'whingeing Jock' behaviour, the sort of comment which is, I would suggest indicative, of the critics' own attitudes to our indigenous culture. I do not think that an Inuit, or a Basque, or a Han, or a San is my cultural inferior, nor that a Parisian, Madrileno (inhabitant of Madrid) or Londoner is any better or worse than me. They have the right to celebrate their own history and culture, as do I.

I would like to draw attention to a particular story in a Kailyard classic. The story is 'The Posty' and the book is Ian MacLaren's *Days of Auld Lang Syne*. The very title reeks of what is portrayed – by those who would convince us they ken best – as sentimentality and nostalgia. However on reading the story itself other things become clear. 'The Posty' concerns a local postman in a rural environment who is very popular, but whose liking for a dram is of some concern to a kirk-like, douce, conforming group of his neighbours, who of course have nothing but his best interests at heart. Such is the Posty's conviviality that he is incapable of turning down the offer of a drink on his rounds – and we should always remember that hospitality is at the very core of Scottish traditional society (along with most other areas of the world uncorrupted by the sanctimoniousness and snobbery of centralising elites). Indeed, he would occasionally be found having a wee rest while delivering the mail on foot, on his allocated round. One after another we are presented with people who gently remonstrate with him about his behaviour and, in each case, quote the Christian bible at him. These people can perhaps be best summed up in Dundee author William Blain's pithy phrase[3] the Richt Yins: those who consider themselves to be the leaders of society, whose veneer of respectability is often no more than an unctuous disguise for naked self-interest. The nub of the story is that the Posty deflects all of their arguments by counter quotations from the same source. As a product of the Scottish Presbyterian education system he is as well-read in terms of the Bible as any of them.

This, I believe, is an incisive, and very funny, comment on precisely the kind of genteel, uncritical and conformist types of thinking that the Kailyard is supposed to represent. It is also more: it is a reflection of Scotland's actual history that the commitment of the post-Reformation Presbyterian church to education for all was a significant and on-going mainstay of Scottish culture. The actions of Knox and his contemporaries in the post-Reformation period have been popularly thought of as expressions of blinkered bigotry. While there definitely was a streak of what our Australian cousins would call wowserism within the Kirk, to concentrate on that to the exclusion of all else misses the point. The ideals of the Presbyterian church were founded in part on the works of George Buchanan (1506-1582) and I would like to quote my friend and colleague Donald Smith on Buchanan:

> (Buchanan's) Dialogue on the Law of Kingship among the Scots was prompted as a defence of the overthrow of a legitimate reigning Queen, and its subsequent influence has been huge. The argument is that rulers and rulers alike are subject to the rule of law, and bound to obey it in the same way. Consequently, while a King is justified in taking strong measures to uphold the law, so his subjects may be justified in defying and even violently dethroning a ruler who is not behaving lawfully. Buchanan at this juncture anticipates the concept of citizen rights, as well as limited or constitutional monarchy. Both come from his dedication to Stoic virtues of reason and discipline, which supposedly flourished in the Roman Republic after Kings and before Emperors.[4]

Buchanan went on to outline a history of Scottish kingship, based on the sovereignty not of the ruler but of the governed, the people. Legitimacy in Scotland, he argued, has always come from below and not above. The idea sees ultimate political authority being rooted in the community of the nation as a whole. It is an idea that may well be tested soon enough.

The idea that everyone should be able to read the Bible for themselves was central to the Presbyterian ideal, which was itself based on a form of communitarianism, the congregation being the community. The story, 'The Posty', exemplifies that aspect of Scottish culture: the injunction that people should, and can, think for themselves. That old line about a Scotsman being someone who can start a fight in a phone-box is rooted in what the historian James D Young rightly celebrated as carnaptiousness – the love of debate. In 'The Posty' we see this in everyday life and the hero's capacity to counter the arguments of those who would control him is a salutary lesson on the independence of thought that is so central to actual Scottish culture. Is it any accident that during most of the nineteenth and twentieth centuries the Scots were the greatest readers of newspapers in the world?

It may also be the case that the original designation of the Kailyard as an inferior genre of literature was partly based on the fact that it was just too Scottish for those who saw themselves as possessing the right to be the arbiters of taste – for all.

As noted, the term Kailyard originally referred to the vegetable garden of most rural Scottish houses. That this term was chosen for this genre of writing was in itself perhaps a sly dig at the blandness and homogeneity of the Scottish diet, and in turn the Scottish way of life, by those caught in the Scottish cringe who are constantly aping those they perceived to be their 'betters'. In that regard it is interesting to note that, like oats, over the past few years kail, or kale, has become something of a hit amongst 'foodies', and again, like oats, is now part that group of foods known as 'superfoods'. Look back through time and you will see that most staple foods are remarkable for their nutritive properties which is exactly why people who understood their own environments and were steeped in their own cultures had made them staples in the first place. And now the metrovincial elites are catching on...

The charge of nostalgia that has been levelled against the Kailyard writers is perhaps true, and little wonder. The presentation of a rural lifestyle, where people lived in small communities, in a healthy, if testing, environment where everyone looked out for each other must have struck a chord in many Scots, including children, who worked obscenely long hours in dangerous and unsanitary factories, many of whom never saw the sun in the winter, and whose diet was often appalling. You could hardly blame anyone in such a situation for seeking escape in literature, if they had the time or energy to actually read that is. There is a recurring Unionist trope that the Scots did well out of the Empire. This is in fact a lie – the reality for the majority of Scots, they or their parents having been removed from a hard, but healthy life on land they had a visceral connection with, ended up in exile or in the factories and the mills of the Industrial Revolution. Those who did well were the sons of the gentry who could obtain office in the bureaucracy of Empire across the Globe. The idea that the children of the hoi polloi had access to such posts is risible, the few exceptions proving the rule. Certainly many Scots saw the world, in the colours of the British Army, and it is not nationalist propaganda to re-state that the Scots regiments were the front-line troops in most of the British Empire's military rape of the planet. The nostalgia of the Kailyard would also have been attractive to the Diaspora, those thousands upon thousands of Scots, Lowland and Highland who were exiled from their beloved land to further the economic interests of the lairds.

It is generally accepted that the origins of the Kailyard school were in William Robertson Nicoll's *British Weekly* magazine, and Nicoll, along with J M Barrie and the Reverend John Watson (Ian Maclaren) were the main writers of the genre. Barrie is still well known, mainly because of Peter Pan, but it is telling that Crockett who was extremely prolific was deeply interested in Scottish history and wrote several historical novels. Just as many periods of Scottish history need re-visiting so there are many aspects of our culture that could do with re-evaluation, and for me the Kailyard is definitely one. The term Kailyard has come to mean the twee, kitsch portrayal of Scots as a bunch of kilt-wearing, haggis-bashing, hooching buffoons inhabiting a poverty-stricken and backward land, but a revisit to the genre it will show that that has never been the case, despite the fantasies of the mainstream British media and their masters.

There is another point to this. If it is true that many commentators were put off by the usage of Scots – this does not apply to Hugh MacDiarmid who was scathing about the Kailyard, but then again he was scathing about an affy lot o things – then this would fit in with another pattern in Scottish society over the past century and a half. The deliberate suppression of both Gaelic and Scots was manifested in the 1872 Education (Scotland) act, where it is explicitly stated that the language of all education was to be English. This suppression of our indigenous languages has had deleterious effects on generations of Scots – to get on you had to abandon not your dialect, but the language of your parents and their kin. All too many Scots know of instances where Gaelic-speaking parents actively discouraged their children from speaking their native tongue, so convinced had they become that its use was a marker of poverty and ignorance. The fact that there are still numpties around who will try to argue in the face of all evidence that Scots isn't actually a language, or that Gaelic should be allowed to die a 'natural death' shows just how deep-rooted the attack on the auld leids have gone. This of course has been made worse by the so-called 'upper classes' use of a strangulated imitation of English RP and the refusal of the patronising BBC, to countenance anything but cut-glass English accents for their presenters till just a few decades ago.

> Deprive the people of their national consciousness, treat them as a tribe and not a nation, dilute their national pride, do not teach their history, propagate their language as inferior, imply they have a cultural void, emphasise their customs are primitive, and dismiss independence as a barbaric anomaly.

Sound familiar? This is not from a secret memo at the British Home Office dealing with uppity natives from Aberdeen or Bulawayo, but are the words of Reinhard Heydrich, arch-propagandist of the Nazi party and a high-ranking Gestapo officer, in the lead up to the annexation of Czechoslovakia. They carry a sad resonance when we think of the treatment of Scottish culture and history under Whitehall.

The level of control suggested by Heydrich requires willing participants within the institutions of state to promulgate such policies. And in Scotland there has been no shortage of them. This from the late educationalist Robbie Robertson:

> Based solely on the Scottish experience, the place of the elite – individuals and institutions – in establishing the value of a language does, however, seem to be of absolutely central significance. Their authority, patronage, and resources are major factors in establishing *their* interests as models for the entire culture

That is from a limited circulation essay entitled *The English Singularity* but in a later piece written for the magazine 'Education in the North' in 1998 he makes things a bit more explicit. Here he is talking about the reactions of the Scottish Consultative Council on the Curriculum to a report put together after a conference on the teaching of Scots language and Scottish History, which they had commissioned:

> It was evident, for example, at the meeting in March, and subsequent correspondence, that Scottish culture and matters of national identity left some members of Council queasy since they had little confidence in them

These members had charge of the teaching of the Curriculum in Scotland. Thankfully things have improved somewhat since then and the current Curriculum for Excellence has begun to address some of the fundamental problems of denying children the knowledge of their own culture, but much remains to be done. All too often politicians are satisfied with bland statements of intent from institutions with a long track record of maintaining what they think of as the status quo to the exception of all else.

Here is a radical thought. Given that they have the democratic mandate of the people of Scotland, the government could insist that matters of policy are implemented by people whose job it is to do just that. All too often our politicians blindly accept advice from people whose entrenched positions are built on resistance to change, not its implementation. The Sir Humphreys of the Whitehall mandarinate have many counterparts within the administration of governance in Scotland, and far too many of them are thirled to ideas of culture and history that should be anathema to the politicians who have the power to hold them to the terms of their all too generous contracts. If you think I am exaggerating the extent of the problem listen in to the occasional foray of BBC Radio Scotland presenters into using Scots – the sound of embarrassed laughter is the backdrop to their attempts at dealing with the reality of a living ancient tongue still spoken by around a third our population. There are nane sae blin as them that willnae see.

To return to 'The Posty'. It could be argued in MacLaren's story that the higher up people think of themselves as being in contemporary society, the stronger the Scottish Cringe runs in them. And this is something I would suggest still rings true today.

1. http://scottishlit.com/?page_id=171
2. Blaustein, R 2003 The *Thistle and the Brier* McFarland, H Jefferson NC p59
3. Blain,W 1947 *Witch's Blood* Hutchinson London
4. McHardy, SA & Smith, D 2014 *Scotland's Democracy Trail* Luath Edinburgh p 55-6
5. https://en.wikipedia.org/wiki/S._R._**Crockett**
6. Roberston, R *The English Singularity - a View from Scotland*
7. "*The Lang Clartie Rigg*" Education in the North, New Series, Number 6 1998

Saints and Stuff

HISTORY IS ALWAYS as much about the present as the past. How we understand the past colours our perception not only of who we are but also how we relate to the institutions of the society in which we live. Heroes of the past are used by all establishments to bolster their own status and power – though it might be better to note that heroes, and villains, of the past are created for the present – what would the world's perception of Hitler be if Germany had not been defeated in WWII? Reference to past heroes gives justification to the role that establishments play in contemporary society and that justification is of more importance than any 'true' representation of the actions of these supposed heroes. In many cases societies call upon mythical beings from the past to give this type of justification and such figures can be powerful indeed.

This can be seen in how monarchs in the British Isles, in both England and Scotland, have utilised the stories of 'King' Arthur in the past, sometimes to try and justify blatant expansionism, as in the case of Edward I of England, or in the case of his opponent Robert I, King of Scots, to resist that expansionism. This role of history has deep roots. In pre-literate societies heroic figures such as Arthur and Finn McCoul were central to the cultures of the peoples among whom those stories were told. It is testament to the psycho-sociological power of such tales that they have continued to inspire people centuries, maybe even millennia after the stories themselves started being told. Human society in the past was essentially similar to today, and heroes from previous times were idealised figures, even if they had originally been relatively ordinary, though possibly extraordinary, people. That process of idealisation amongst pre-literate peoples is matched precisely by the propagandising aspects of much of our history. To recognise this is not necessarily to make a value judgement about those who created the histories we use to build our own versions of the past. The scribes of the Christian Church who created the annals that are the basis for the development of literate history throughout the West were driven by their own beliefs, and doing the work of God, for them, did not include the concept of 'objective representation of reality'. However, once you recognise that history is developed from such sources and that they must be seen in a critical light, many assumptions can fall.

In a world where nations states dominate, one of the historical processes that can be seen as performing the same function as the stories of heroic figures like Arthur and Fionn is the adoption of a national patron saint among the Christian countries of the world. Scotland's patron saint is St Andrew, a figure of major importance in the Christian story. He is said to have been one of the twelve apostles of Christ, but his link with Scotland is tenuous to put it mildly. Medieval legend states that St Regulus arrived on the east coast of Fife in the fourth century from Patras in Greece carrying with him the relics of St Andrew.[1] Those relics were supposedly three finger bones and a tooth. It is known that many other places claimed in the past to have such relics of St Andrew, leading to the well-known comment that St Andrew had more bones than a herring. Be that as it may, such ideas were common in early Christianity and the legitimacy that relics gave to new church foundations was of considerable importance.

The role of St Andrew was further enhanced by the story told about a battle between the combined Picts and Scots and an invading Northumbrian army in 832. The Northumbrians, led by their king, Athelesan, greatly outnumbered the combined force. They site for the inevitable battle was carefully chosen: a ford on the river Peffer, near the village now known as

Athelstaneford, in East Lothian. The evening before the battle the Picts and Scots were lined up in ranks and led in prayer by their respective kings and their accompanying priests. At that point it was noticed that in the clear blue skies above them clouds had formed in the shape of a diagonal cross. On asking what this was, the Pictish king was told by one of the priests that this was the shape of the cross on which St Andrew had been martyred and that it was sign of his blessing. This idea soon spread through the ranks and encouraged the Pictish and Scottish warriors so much that the following day they inflicted a famous victory over the Northumbrians, slaughtering most of their army. Or so the story goes.

It is said to be because of this that the Saltire was adopted as Scotland's flag. It is a nice story and as the whole point of having a patron saint is to provide both a kind of rallying point and a veneer of Christian respectability, St Andrew appears to have been a shoo-in.

That the original tale is a monkish creation now seems obvious but history is a malleable process. Although St Andrew became Scotland's patron saint this process of adapting the past for political reasons applies even more to Scotland's most famous saint, though again he was not born here. This is St Columba, some of whose bones were said to have been carried before Scottish troops in battle in the Brecbennach, a chapel-shaped reliquary, generally against invaders from the south. The Monymusk Reliquary[2] has been said to be this sacred object but absolute proof is lacking.

The idea of carrying some of the remnants of a corpse for protection in battle may seem strange to some of us today, but this was part of early Christian belief and in it we perhaps see something else of Columba. In Bede's *History of the English Church and People* he quotes a letter from Pope Gregory instructing the English bishop Mellitus to take over the pagan precincts for preaching the word of god. He further orders that the idols of the pagans should be thrown away and destroyed, but can be replaced by the relics of Christian saints –which are apparently Christian idols? The practicality of the idea of taking over the pagan precincts is obvious. The place where people had been gathering for rituals for generations, perhaps even millennia, would provide a good location to give out the new message. This hints at the possibility of certain interesting social continuities to which we will return.

In a world where religion no longer has an automatic hold on all societies it is perhaps too easy to be critical of certain aspects of this idea. Even within apparently secular societies, there are still many political leaders who aspire to a veneer of religious respectability while pursuing policies that directly contravene the basic tents of the religion they pretend to adhere to – Theodious Blair being a fine example. The behaviour of generations of British government ministers in happily promoting the sale of weapons of all kinds to bloodthirsty dictators and psychopathic regimes around the world is obvious. War is, after all, the most profitable export of them all – guns always need bullets.

The idea of the patron saint developed long ago and in Scotland, St Columba has been regularly presented through the years as 'the Dove of the Church', a clear attempt to portray him as a man of peace and an essentially gentle soul. From the little evidence that does exist he was neither. And this evidence comes from others within the ranks of the same religion as himself. Part of the problem is that so much of our early history can only be gleaned from the writings of monks whose objective was the glorification of their idea of Godhead and the furthering of the interests of their religion, rather than presenting an accurate picture of what had happened in times gone by.

The use of the Brecbennach underlines Columba's position as a quasi-patron saint, it was clearly seen as offering some sort of protection as well as legitimacy. The question has to be asked, who was this Columba. The main source for information about Columba is his *Life* written by Adomnan, one of his successors as Abbot of Iona more than a hundred years after Columba died. The word hagiography was invented to describe writing the life of a saint but it has come to have another broader meaning which is a biography that puts the subject in a flattering light. You would expect no less from Adomnan, who, like Columba, was Abbot of Iona, and most of the *Life* is devoted to describing the miracles, good works and the essential sanctity of Columba. He makes no mention of aspects of Columba's life before he came to Scotland, which shed an altogether less flattering light on the man. Nor does he mention the companions of Columba who other early sources tell were with him on many important occasions.

In Ireland, where he was and is still known as Columcille, he was a priest of some renown. It seems he borrowed a psalter or prayer-book, from another priest at called Fintan. He then copied the manuscript and in those days before printing was invented this led to a problem.[3] Fintan had not given permission for this copy to be made and demanded Columba give him the copy. In this we can see that there was a level of competitiveness amongst the Christian clergy of the time. If they were all simply doing God's work together, what should it matter? It may have been simply that Fintan was annoyed that Columba had not had the good grace to ask his permission but subsequent events suggest there was more to this than simple pique. Columba refused to hand over the book and the matter was taken before an ecclesiastic court. There the judgement was given the 'the calf goes with the cow', meaning that because Columba had not asked for permission, the copy belonged to Fintan. The language of the judgement reflects the reality that the manuscript was made of calfskin.

This did not please Columba who was a leading member of the Ui Neill clan – the early British churches were attached to local tribes and were to some extent part of their wider social organization – and he called on his kinfolk to support him. This put him in direct conflict with the other priests who likewise called on their own kin for support. At this point in Ireland, and perhaps in Scotland, such Christian establishments were known as *muinntirs* or brotherhoods of the land. There was no definitive hierarchical structure to the organisations, each individual community being led by its own abbot, and Columba was defending his own position through his kin. In the ensuing battle at Cul Dremne many men were killed, estimates going as high as 3000. The upshot of this was that Columba was expelled from Ireland, some saying that he was sent off to find as many converts for the Christian religion as he had caused to be killed in the battle. These are not the actions of a man of peace, This is a man who will not be told what to do.

So he was sent off to Scotland, where there had been earlier missionaries, St Ninian over a century earlier is believed by many people to have converted some of the tribes in Scotland but most references tell that they had subsequently given up Christianity. However, in the sixth century there were other Irish monks who records suggest had gone to Scotland, but most are now almost forgotten.

Once Columba was ensconced in Iona, with the permission of the locals – the muinntir idea would not have been unknown to the Scottish tribes of Dalriada – he began to involve himself in politics. Even in the pages of Adomnan's *Life* it is clear that his actions involving the kingship of Dalriada were extremely political. He is said to have become involved in securing the election of the king Aedan MacGabhran as king of Dalriada. I am of the opinion that the use of the term king to describe the figurehead of a confederation of tribal peoples, which the Scots of Dalriada, like their cousins the Picts, undoubtedly were, to be anachronistic. It is a word that the early Christian scribes used of all such cases, but that should not delude us into thinking that these were kings like the Biblical and Classical ones who had been part of the education of the monks. Nor should they be thought of as being in any way like the feudalised monarchs of later England, or their counterparts north of the border.

The simplification of history is often a smokescreen and seeing all early leaders as being just like later kings can be seen as an elitist distortion of reality. Be that as it may, Columba actively intervened in the election of a new king and it seems his chosen candidate Aedan became 'king'. That this was probably down to Aedan's support of Christianity need not be discussed here, but it helps paint a picture of Columba being as proud and manipulative as he was when he caused the trouble in Ireland. A gentle, unassuming man of peace he was not, and it is tempting to think that if his exile had taught him anything it was to look out for the main chance.

By the time Adomnan had become Abbot of Iona he was no longer just the successor of Columba. He had firmly hitched his cart to the new developments in Christianity. At the Synod of Whitby in 664, under the cover of supposedly discussing the differences in when and how the insular British church and the Church of Rome celebrated Easter, and how their monks shaved their hair, Cuthbert, a Northumbrian bishop had made a clever and highly effective power play.[4] By accepting the rule of the Church of Rome in such matters, the effective independence of the insular or Celtic church, where they were allied to their own kin on their own tribal territory, was superseded by the dominance of the hierarchical power of Rome. Bishops in the insular church were officiants who ordained new priests, but in the Roman Church they were an integral part of its centralized, and centralizing, power structure. Along with this power play there was what can be seen as a land grab. There would have been no need for the *muinntirs* to have specified ownership of the lands they used - they were part of the wider, tribal community.

Now they would be under the rule of the Roman Church, and it is salutary to notice just how closely the pattern of Church rule followed the administrative structures of the Roman Empire. Their lands were effectively ceded over to a foreign power. And Adomnan was central to this, for in his hagiography of Columba he was presenting a unifying figure for the Christians amongst the Picts, Scots and Britons of Scotland. Thus, the tale of Columba as the man who Christianized Scotland was born and the church of Iona became the mother church of Scotland, but as an integral part of the Roman structure. It is from this particular set of circumstances that the move towards making Columba our most famous saint most likely grew. As scribes, the Christian clergy were very useful to the centralizing leaders of the various Scottish tribal confederations as they sought to defend themselves against first Northumbrian and later, Viking and English attempts to conquer the peoples of Scotland from the seventh century on. This put the church right at the heart of power, and able to influence just how history was presented, something also helped by the fact that initially they were the only sector of society that was literate. This process saw most high-level administrators of European nation states being clerics for centuries, and Scotland was no exception.

Columba may have been an arrogant and overly-forceful character, and a man unafraid to shed blood, but the story of his peaceful Christianization of Scotland is one which was developed by the Church for its own purposes. In far too many countries across the globe we have seen that religious change is often very bloody indeed, and there are no good reasons for thinking that things were different here apart from the official line which has worked so well. When we look at what happened elsewhere in Europe as Christianity expanded it is obvious that in many cases this was a brutal process. During the expansion of the European Empires across the globe in the seventeenth and eighteenth centuries, Christianity was spread, as the old cliché has it, with the Bible in one hand and the sword in the other. The imposition of the religion in Scandinavia nearly a thousand years earlier had likewise been a brutal and bloody affair. Yet Scotland is supposed to have been different. We have no records that tell of such brutality but the only records we have are those of the priests themselves, and it is not good historical practice to build a case on a single source, or in this case multiple sources all from the same organisation. And those records tell us of only one Scottish martyr, St Donnan, supposedly killed on the orders of a local queen in the early seventh century.[5]

The hold of religion on the body politic, and its attraction to those in charge, is still with us but I would suggest that here in Scotland the story presented is very much open to challenge. We should also bear in mind that our universities were set up not as havens for seekers of truth, but as training colleges for the clergy.

For a very long time indeed our history was in the hands of those who were exclusively believers in the Christian concept of a masculine God and Father. The portrayal of women throughout much of Christianity's history, as the source of all sin, is clearly borderline madness, but it is an idea that still has a strong hold in many religions, whose absolute gynophobia is in itself an an ongoing problem for many societies. Here I am not talking of faith – what you believe is your own business – but organised and structured religion. One simply has to think of the internecine wars between sects of Christians and Muslims to see the problem. That such schismatic differences are of use to the powerful and psychopathic seeking control over others is also blindingly obvious. Slaughtering children in the name of a loving God says it all.

But back to Columba, he was a useful tool not only for the increasingly centralizing monarchs of Scotland from the time of David I on, but also to the church. Their idea of Iona as Scotland's mother church was an echo of how Rome liked to present itself and the notion of the family of Iona was built up over centuries. Its effects have been varied. Some early Presbyterians took to arguing that the Presbyterian church, with its emphasis on the community of the congregation, was the true natural successor to the insular British, or Columban church. Their argument was that as that church arose outwith the control of the Church of Rome, they themselves could claim to be true heirs of the original British church. This was, if convoluted, definitely carnaptious to a particularly Scottish degree! But the concentration on Columba and Iona, ignores the role of other supposed early saints who were here both before and alongside him.

One such figure was St Colm, said to have come from Ireland along with the monks Fergus and Merchard, who were also to become saints, and to whom many early churches appear to have been originally dedicated. Later historians appear to have happily lumped all such dedications in with those to Columba to help big him up. It is important not to make too much of a value judgement on this as most of those actually writing things down did have a belief that they were doing the right thing, certainly on behalf of their own religion. They were also often doing so at the behest of others further up the system. A great deal of evil has been perpetrated by those claiming to be followers of a just, kind, or loving god in mankind's story this far.

In *Scotland's Future History* I mentioned the power that literature gave to the Early Church. I also noted that stories can survive over remarkable periods of time. One of the side effects of Columba becoming such a dominant figure in Scotland's story is that little attention has been paid to many of the supposed early saints of Scotland. In his book *Kalendars of Scottish Saints* 1872, Bishop Forbes gave details of many such now-forgotten characters, many of whom appear to have been Christianised versions of individuals, and even of groups who appear to have originally been pre-Christian like the Nine Maidens already mentioned. In different ways, the Nine Maidens and the buildings at the Ness of Brodgar show us that this part of the world was never a backwater before being made so by an unfortunate political union. And for a patron saint I would prefer the thoroughly mythical Jock Tamson, who was father to us all, even if he is known by different names in other societies.

1. http://omniumsanctorumhiberniae.blogspot.
   co.uk/2015/11/saint-regulus-and-relics-of-saint-andrew.
   html
2. http://www.nms.ac.uk/explore/stories/scottish-history-
   and-archaeology/monymusk-reliquary/
3. https://opensource.com/law/11/6/story-st-columba-
   modern-copyright-battle-sixth-century-ireland
4. https://www.britannica.com/event/Synod-of-Whitby
5. http://www.oldenglishchurch.org.uk/saint-donnan/

Stories and Histories

IN SCOTLAND TODAY, genealogy is big business, with vast amounts of collated data on computers, genealogical societies and groups in many parts of the country and an increasing, if rather unfortunate rush to tie DNA analysis into the concept of personal and family history. Only a couple of hundred years ago such interest in genealogy was different. Every clan – a Scottish Gaelic term meaning tribe – had its own *seannachie*, a man among whose duties was the recitation of the traditional ancestry of the clan, back to its founder, whenever there was a major public event. People in the Highland society that survived to the eighteenth century were as tied to this idea of knowing your own family story as their ancestors had been back in the Iron Age and before, and as so many of their descendants are today. The need to know where you come from is deep in all of us.

But story is so much more than genealogy or even history. History can be described as the act of telling the past in terms of 'Big Men doing Big Things'. As such it is more to do with preserving the power of elites than giving an accurate picture of the past for most people. As I have noted above, it is a truism that the winners write history, but, even so, the losers do not become mute. The process of history being about Big Men doing Big Things has been perpetuated by the universities who tend to have a particular, and I would suggest somewhat blinkered, view of scholarship, though things are improving in some areas. It is a view of scholarship that is absolutely rooted in literacy and I would go so far as to say that we should be wary of the incipient tyranny of literacy. This is not to reject literacy – that would appear a little self-defeating given you are reading my words off this page – but that we have to be wary of all forms of information. Long before history began to be put onto the page – and there can be some discussion of when exactly that was, given that so much of what is used as historical resource is unashamedly propagandistic material – before literacy was invented people told at least some of their stories to do just what history sets out to do. That is to provide an intellectual, and emotional framework that allows people to understand their place in the world. That was a basic keystone of the storytelling process for the millennia that humans inhabited this planet before writing came along.

Before writing, all knowledge had to be passed on either by example or by spoken explanation. This encompassed all aspects of human existence, as it was imperative to explain to the growing generation how to live in an ever-uncertain world. Behind the nursery tales of princesses and princes lie social and psychological realities that lay at the heart of all knowledge and education in oral communities. The fact that so many stories actually involve so-called princesses and princes may in fact be more to do with literacy and the expectations it arouses than the originals of the stories themselves.

As an instance of this, the well-known story of the Princess and the Frog in which the youngest of three sisters eventually releases a handsome Prince from his enchantment as a frog, has the sisters going to the well to draw water for their mother. This is not, and never has been a role that any princess would have undertaken, seeing as the fundamental role of royalty has always been to try and show that they are not like anyone else and in fact are 'better' than the rest of us, and require servants to fulfil those tasks which the rest of us accept as daily necessity. Look, and you will find many such examples. It is essentially a process of gentrification of popular culture.

In non-literate societies, and some still exist today, stories encompass all life and serve to continually reinforce the bonds of community that were so necessary in environments less technically restricted than today and thus more volatile. They were also the primary means of education for the young.

On long, cold, dark winter nights in Scotland, as elsewhere, families and groups of families gathered round the flickering hearth fires to listen to tales whose relevance to their way of life was absolute. Those who had the gift of storytelling were bearers not just of tradition but of knowledge, artists as well as entertainers, and today, through the power of the spoken word, the magic of ancient themes re-worked have not lost their power. Stories told by the fireside centuries ago on the far side of the earth can surface today in modern industrial urban garb, and though many tales from many lands in many tongues are now available in books, such stories are like musical notation – a place to start, but not the thing itself! Even today in our ever more electronic world, stories are being told that have probably never been written down, some from ancient sources, others as fresh as tomorrow's bread and others still reworked from tradition and reborn. All come from the same well.

And drinking from that well starts early. Before children acquire language they are exposed to story in various forms. In most societies this will consist of children being told stories or sung songs, often to help them go to sleep. This is how basic socialisation starts, with children hearing not just random conversation but structured language tailored to make a point – to tell a story. Sadly this does not happen to every child; leaving aside those born deaf, even in some of the most wealthy societies on our planet, there are children brought up in such deprivation that they are not exposed to this process, often with devastating results for both them and the communities they inhabit. I think it fair to say that the centrality of storytelling is close to a human norm. Children will be spoken to in order to start them on their journey of growing into their own potential. I only know of my own experience but I cannot recall how many times I have heard, or said myself, the words, 'Oh that's a great story' or 'Go on tell us story' to an infant making her or his first attempts to create coherent sounds, on the way to acquiring spoken language. This use of story, and song, is what mothers, and fathers, grandmothers and grandfathers, have learned to do over untold millennia and I doubt it is much different from human behaviour in the earliest Stone Age when humans were beginning to develop into what we now think of as ourselves. That process too was aided by story.

Children respond to stories. Particularly stories that have stood the test of time, and it is a recurring experience for a storyteller to be asked by a group of children he or she has not seen in months, or even years, to tell the story they last heard her or him tell. This need for repetition is an aspect of story that appears to fulfil a basic need. It is part of the storytelling process that the teller and the audience become, at least for a while, an integrated community. The sharing of the story demands this. Later I will look at how this function actually works but suffice it to say here that children like repetition. Even if a child is read a story, it is often the same story that they want. The repetition brings comfort, through the familiarity of both the words and the cadences of the teller. And as the *seannachies* of old could not make a mistake in their recitation of the clan's genealogy – most of their audience would know it very well indeed – so the child wants the story just the same – you change it at your peril! This does not matter quite so much when dealing with groups of children, but as individuals they like to hear the story just the way they like it, and are used to. In this there is some kind of sophisticated psychological process taking place, I am sure, and again I think it is rooted in the very concept of socialisation – teaching a child how to live as a human within the community he or she is going to inhabit. For it is within the community that the story really works. Communal experience is the well from which story arises.

And that well is deep. Stories only survive because they fill a need – social, psychological or a combination of these and just as we are basically little different from our ancestors of thousands of years ago – apart perhaps from our technological invention and disregard for the health of our environment - so stories which enthral, excite and educate us are in their essentials probably little different from tales they told. After all, life, death, love and the need to work to eat are fundamental to humanity the world over in all time. And some tales come from time beyond all measure. The indigenous people of Australia still tell of their ancestors hunting giant animals, known to western scientists as Diprotodons,[1] more than twenty or even thirty thousand years ago. The knowledge of these animals, and of major geophysical events like volcanoes and tsunamis was passed down through oral transmission, generation to generation over many millennia. From the tongue to the ear.

All storytellers have a favourite story, some particularly inventive and talented storytellers have only the one story, which they can adjust and recalibrate to every occasion. I first heard my own favourite story over forty years ago and through retelling it so often it has become an integral part of my life. I am also reminded every time I tell it of something that Picasso said. 'It took me years to learn to paint like a master, but a lifetime to paint like a child'. He was surely suggesting that what was important was to be as open-minded and as intellectually absorbent as a child when it comes to the creative process. There are some aspects of specific oral traditions – the genealogies recited by the *seannachies* are a case in point, as are stories linked with rituals – where specific repetition is called for. But, I believe the key to telling a story, or singing a song, is just as it was said in Scots by the great ballad singer Mrs Frances Brown of Falkland in the 1840s: 'To mak it new'[2]. Every time she sang a song she was effectively re-inventing it. Her description of the process makes it clear she knew the tune, and the story and a set of phrases and ideas that could be understood as a kind of grammar of song. Strangely this process works even with children – as long as you don't change the basics of the story you can say and do a lot to ensure, on the day and in the place where you tell the story, that the story lives. To tell stories as if reading from a book can be little more than shallow antiquarianism. The teller must feel the story so the audience can too, and to some extent this is best done by allowing the story to be told through you rather than trying to dictate the story. This is not true in all cultures and numerous storytellers in the world today are more like actors with a script, but many traditional storytellers mak it new every time.

What has this to do with history? Quite a lot. As I have noted above the old cliché about history being written by winners is evidently true but what do those who are 'losers' do? Do they run away and shut up, letting the story that the winners tell become the accepted truth? This might well be the case if the only people who matter are those who see themselves as elites – they tell and re-tell their versions of the past to each other with enthusiasm. They also ensure that their version of events is the one that is taught in schools, and universities. But many losers in any struggle carry on living, and unless their culture is eradicated they will tell stories. Outside of the classroom or the lecture theatre, in the home, in the workplace, in the pub or at the match, other versions of the past survive.

In Scotland this has specific resonance in the late Jacobite period where both song and story demonstrate the effect that the cause of Jacobitism continued, and continues, to have on the Scottish psyche. And because this has survived generally outwith accepted cultural mores it has depths of meaning that can be surprising. Apart from the undoubted fact of ethnic cleansing and a decade long military occupation of most of Scotland after Culloden, the reality of what Jacobitism was to those who supported it, as opposed to the Stewarts themselves, is something that is made manifest in the very survival of the songs and stories. The continuing hold that such material has had on the Scots psyche is reflective, not of support for the Stewart Dynasty and its aspirations to power, but of something much more visceral.

Being someone who grew up with nothing but disdain for Bonnie Prince Charlie I have to say that studying the Jacobite period over many years has led me to change my opinion of him, if not about what he represented, or his political ambitions. I am not nor ever have been any kind of Royalist – I consider the very idea of kings and their ilk offensive, a form of hopefully soon-doomed sociological and political sickness – but I have come to terms with the fact that Charles Edward Stewart was a brave, talented, charismatic individual and worthy of some respect. He was still a prince, with all that entails, but the support he got – nobody grassed him up when he was on the run even though the money on offer was the equivalent in modern terms of several million pounds – was remarkable. His continuing hold on the Scottish psyche is because of what he represented, not who, or what he was. The Jacobite cause from the very beginning was, I believe, defined in Scotland by an extreme reluctance to accept the idea of Union. This also explains why the Jacobites have continued to fascinate so many Scots. They echo remembrance of a time before Union, and though this is in part nostalgic it is also a recognition that the ancient country of Scotland was sold down the river by 'a parcel of rogues'. Even the arch-establishment Walter Scott could not entirely eradicate his own sympathies for the Jacobites and, despite his acceptance of entrenched power, he was man who was steeped in the history and culture of Scotland. I suspect he must have been, in modern terms, a bit conflicted.

One particular story I came across concerns the killing of a couple of Redcoats sometime after Culloden. They were molesting a young woman when two Highlanders driving their cattle to Rannoch moor, where they would be safe from the British Army's rapacity, passed by. When they intervened the soldiers turned on them and in the ensuing struggle the soldiers were killed, and buried in unmarked graves. The story no doubt played well amongst a population who had been subjected to rape and pillage on an industrial scale by the

British Army (with several Scots to the fore) but to accept it as true without corroboration is no more intellectually sound than accepting a single literary source as reliable history. We have to be critical of story just as we have to be critical of history – but in a different way.

I mentioned earlier that I tell students that the most useful tool in history is the Latin phrase *cui bono* – who profits. This means that you have to look at the beliefs of, and understand the point of view of, whoever is writing any particular history at any given time, to try and discern whether or not they have a particular motive in presenting the version of history they are writing. Nowadays we can see that the early writing of Christian monks have to be treated with care but for centuries their word was – almost – taken as Gospel, because of the dominance of Christianity in Scottish life and culture. But this approach does not work for story; the very fact that a story survives shows that it has value to the community in which it is told but who first told it cannot be known. It's survival shows that whoever originally told it gave something of value to the community. Its survival gives it validity but story is not concerned with the practicalities of history as reportage. It is concerned with what resonates with the audience – it plays to their ideas and beliefs.

Sometimes story can lead to specific historical sources. In *Scotland's Future History* I mentioned the Cantonment Register of the British Army 1746-53, to which I was led by following up material about Iain Dubh Cameron, the Serjeant Mor. The evidence in that document about the garrisoning of Scotland is dramatic but it also raises a question. Are there other such documents that directly contradict the history we are given? There does not seem to be a publicly accessible copy of George Mealmaker's *Moral and Political Catechism of Man* (1797) in Scotland (see below) and you will also look in vain for access to the Stuart Papers, the documents relating to the Stuart dynasty in Scotland. The original collection is at

Windsor Castle, but microfiche copies do exist in libraries in Australia and the USA. I am not suggesting that all such circumstances are the result of conspiracy, but the notion that Scottish history, and thus Scotland, is only of secondary interest at best is part of the mentality of those who I have been calling Gatekeepers. It is one with the recurring trope, beloved of our mainstream media that Scotland is 'too wee and too poor' to go it alone, ignoring the reality that there are many successful nation states smaller than us.

One of the ways that the Gatekeeper mentality directly affects history is the recurring notion that the Scots are as much to blame for everything that happened in our history as the English/British. By this way of thinking the brutal activities of Captains Caroline Scott of the British Army and James Fergusson of the Navy in the violent ethnic cleansing post-Culloden in some way make all Scots guilty.[3] To me this is like blaming all Norwegians for the activities of the pro-Nazi government led by Hermann Quisling from 1942-45. It is an attempt to deflect attention away from the fact that it was government policy for the British Army to rape, loot and pillage through the Highlands after Culloden, as is well documented in the *The Lyon in Mourning*,[3] the material for which was collected from the late 1740s through to the 1770s, but tellingly was not published until 1834 (from which you can draw your own conclusions). This vast array of primarily eye-witness evidence is still ignored by some historians who claim there was no ethnic cleansing in the Highlands. Anger against such behaviour should be tempered by pity for such people whose blinkered thinking rejects evidence when it conflicts with their political views. If you wish to attribute more nefarious motives to such activities that is entirely up to you but I do think that many such commentators simply do not want to face up to such evidence precisely because it could undermine their adherence to what can be referred to as Received Opinion, or the establishment party line.

The Radical 1790s

LAST YEAR SAW a welcome series of events to celebrate the 250th anniversary of the birth of Thomas Muir (1765-1799), the lawyer from Huntershill, who was one of the leading lights of the reform movement in the early 1790s in Scotland. While this is a step in the right direction, we should be careful not to fall into thinking that history is only about notable individuals. This is an easy trap to fall into but the idea that it is only individuals that change history is truly a dangerous one. In this respect the words of the English playwright and poet Willie Shakespeare ring true when he said 'cometh the hour, cometh the man'. Certainly leaders are necessary but they can only be effective if they are part of something much bigger than themselves. So while Muir was undoubtedly a charismatic and talented man he was by no means a lone figure and it is important that we remember there were many others involved in the agitation of the times. Due to the fact that the Scottish Societies of the Friends of the People had membership fees of several pennies, unlike the similar societies in England where such fees were numbered in guineas, this meant that a broad section of society was involved in the reform movement here; a fact that only increased the paranoia of the Establishment. Muir was transported with four companions who, like him, had been subjected to show trials for their activities. Those companions were Joseph Gerrald, Thomas Fysshe Palmer, Maurice Margarot, and William Skirving, and it is a reflection of how far we have yet to go in truly coming to terms with our nation's past that there is still no mention of the Political Martyr's Monument to them in Calton Cemetery on the noticeboard at the cemetery gate (can anyone hear a bee buzzing...). Although they are generally known as the Scottish Political Martyrs, due to them being tried in, and transported from, Scotland,, in fact only Muir and Skirving were Scottish. Their arrests, show trials and subsequent transportation wre ortchestrated by Henry Dundas, Lord Melville (1742-1811), a leading member of Pitt's Tory government in the 1790s whose single-handed control over Scotland in the 1790s was tyrannical.

Joseph Gerrald (1763-1796) had been born to a wealthy Irish father in the West Indies. Before moving to London for his education. He worked as a lawyer in Philadelphia in the 1780s before moving to London, where he became active in advocating Reform. He, along with Margarot, attended the 1793 British Convention of Delegates of the People as a delegate from London.

Thomas Fysshe Palmer (1747-1802) was a Unitarian minister who came from the upper strata of English society and had attended Eton and Cambridge, but had become disillusioned with a political system he considered corrupt. Through the 1780s he preached in a variety of Scottish East Coast towns and came to the fore in Radical agitation in Dundee in the early 1790s.

Maurice Margarot (1745-1815) was a London born wine merchant who had been educated on the Continent and his support of the French Revolution led to him becoming one of the founders of the London Corresponding Society in 1792 This was an organisation which, like the various Friends of the People groups, called for peaceful democratic reform. Like Gerrald, he was a fine public speaker, and this was probably the reason he was chosen as a target for persecution.

Like the others, William Skirving (1745-1796) was not from a particularly humble background. A farmer's son, he had been born at Liberton and had gone to university with the initial intention of becoming a minister but instead became a tutor for a while, after which he followed his father into farming. Caught up in the new ideas of his time in agriculture as well as politics, he published a book called *The Husbandman's Assistant* in 1792. Since the mid '70s he had been farming in Fife and had become closely involved with Palmer and George Mealmaker through Radical activities in Dundee.

The significance of this group can be seen in the raising of the Monument to them in Calton Cemetry, on Edinburgh's Waterloo Place, in the 1840s, after the passing of the Great Reform Act of 1832 which greatly extended the right to vote. Their role in the agitation to extend suffrage was well understood at the time – the monument being raised by public subscription – even if subsequently they became almost totally forgotten.

Even before these five men had been put on trial, the show trials had begun. The first to have been put on trial was in fact James Tytler (1745-1804), a man whose erudition and wide interests made him uniquely representative of his times.[1] Although most commentators in the Enlightenment period in Scotland emphasise the creativity and innovation of contemporary thought, as Tytler's experience shows, there were very strong limits on just how far creativity and innovation could go. And one place they could not go was into the field of politics. Far too many of the *philosophes* who many claim were responsible for the creation of the modern world were not willing or able to challenge the political status quo. Tytler was one of the exceptions. He was instrumental in the creation of the second and third editions of the Encyclopaedia Britannica, worked as a pharmacist and had an abiding interest in the ultra-modern field of Aviation. In 1784 he became the second man to fly in a balloon in Britain, one month after his rival Vincenzo Lunardi had taken to the skies over London.

A man of strong political views, Tyler had great sympathy with the French Revolution of 1789 and in the early 1790s published a couple of pamphlets attacking the corruption of the British Parliament. This was deemed sedition by the authorities and he was put on trial in 1793. One of the seditious libels he was charged with publishing ended: 'If the king hear you not, keep your money in your pockets, and frame your laws, and the minority must submit to the majority'. Dangerous stuff indeed. And when he failed to appear at his trial in January he was outlawed, leaving surreptitiously for Belfast before making his way to America where his new role as a newspaper publisher saw him come to the notice of the authorities there. During his voyage to America he wrote another pamphlet attacking the corrupt elite called *Rising of the sun in the west, or the Origin and progress of liberty*.

He was not the only Radical to flee to America, and a great deal of research remains to be done in this area. Another who fled was someone who clearly shows that nationalism is nothing new in Scotland. This was James Thomson Callender (1758-1803), a clerk at the Sasines office who in 1792 produced a work called *The Political Progress of Great Britain*.[2] This is an excoriating attack on the corruption of the British state and its rapaciousness in the expansion of its global empire. It also details the author's analysis of just how Westminster control had impoverished the majority of the population in both Scotland and Ireland. Moderate it is not, but much of it is detailed and accurate, and there is no doubt that he saw England as the cause of most of Scotland's problems. He was a fierce and often vituperative writer and at one point, no doubt full of enthusiasm caused by the growing support for democratic ideals in Scotland, he writes, 'A revolution will take place in Scotland before the lapse of ten years at farther, most likely much sooner'. A man who was known to be fond of the bottle, Callender was incapable of moderation but his criticism of entrenched corruption was well-researched and trenchant. So trenchant in fact that the publication was banned and he realised that he was in danger. Accordingly, he fled to America where he is famous, or notorious, for his role in the vicious inter-party newspaper wars of the late 1790s. In fact, many believe it was his writings that led to the Sedition Act of 1798 which saw him being locked up in the Land of the Free, basically for his uncontrolled, some did say unhinged, attacks on the Democratic Party. A troublesome man, he was eventually pardoned when the Republican Thomas Jefferson became President in 1802 and the act was rescinded. He continued to be a thorn in just about everybody's side till his death in 1803.

In total, there were twenty two trials for sedition in Scotland between 1793 and 1820, illustrating the reality that the country was in much more of a ferment than historians have been prepared to acknowledge.

One of those put on trial was George Mealmaker (1768-1808) a Dundee weaver who had formed the Dundee Friends of Liberty with Thomas Fysshe Palmer in the 1780s. In the early 1790s he wrote a pamphlet *The Dundee Address to the Friends of Liberty* (1793) criticising the despotism of the British government. Palmer was put on trial in 1794 for distributing this pamphlet so it was obviously only a matter of time before Mealmaker had his collar felt by Dundas's minions. However it took them several years, a period in which Mealmaker joined the Society of United Scotsmen, a more radical organisation than the Friends of the People or the Friends of Liberty. This organisation was modelled to some extent on the Society of United Irishmen, who were to the fore in the abortive Irish uprising against British rule in 1798.

Mealmaker wrote another piece, *The Moral and Political Catechism of Man,* in 1797, which strongly advocated annual parliaments and universal suffrage, key ideas in Radical thinking of the time. As noted above, to date, I have been unable to access a copy of this work anywhere in Scotland, which seems illustrative of just how politicised our history has been. In 1798 he was arrested, tried, found guilty and transported for 14 years to Botany Bay. Mealmaker had been heavily involved in Dundee in 1793 when a Tree of Liberty was planted.[3] This was something that happened in many towns and cities at the time and was a deliberate echo of the Establishment practice of erecting a tree to mark some notable event like the birth of a Royal or a military victory. In Dundee, as elsewhere, this lead to a riot and the calling out of troops. The tree itself was uprooted but re-planted on the quiet by Reformers. In Australia, Mealmaker prospered for a while. His weaving skills were of value to the colony but after his small factory burnt down in 1807 his life changed, for the worse, and he died in poverty a year later.

One of the judges at Mealmaker's trial was the notorious Robert McQueen, Lord Braxfield (1722-1799). Incidentally, why are judges given titles that ape the aristocracy? At the trial of Gerrald in 1794 when the defendant remarked that many great men had been reformers, including Jesus Christ, Braxfield jokingly murmured in a stage whisper, 'Muckle he made o that, he was hangit'. We should perhaps remember that Law is not the same thing as Justice and rarely, if ever, has been under any system of centralized government.

The Radical agitation of the 1790s also saw the government's use of *agents provocateurs*. This type of activity, along with infiltration by spies, has long been a useful tool for those in power, as has recently been seen in the scandalous behaviour of undercover policemen even having families with members of anti-war groups in the UK. At a time when there are actual threats to the lives of the population from various fanatic groups it is an illustration of the on-going paranoia of the British powers that be regarding any organised anti-establishment activity, or what they perceive as such. The waste of scarce resources in infiltrating openly democratic, pacifist groups when there are nutters building bombs is a perfect illustration of both the paranoia and the political myopia of the British ruling class.

Probably the most famous of the *agents provocateurs* of the 1790s was Robert Watt, who had offered his services to Henry Dundas as a spy amongst the Friends of the People.[4] A local wine merchant, Watt seems to have seen his activities primarily as a way of earning money. Possibly as a result of no longer being paid for his services as a spy, Watt seems to have become a bit overenthusiastic in his activities. With David Downie he formed a shadowy organisation called the Committee of Ways and Means along with a handful of others. They laid plans for an actual uprising and even went so far as to have pikes made, but as the Committee never numbered even a dozen men the whole affair seems pathetic. This would appear to be just what Dundas wanted and when the pikes were found, both Watt and Downie were arrested and charged with treason. The affair may have been a bit more serious had they been stockpiling firearms. Their trial ran from August into September in 1794, and the upshot was they were both found guilty and sentenced to death – to be executed in the traditional manner for traitors of being hung, drawn and quartered. In fact, Downie was pardoned for turning King's evidence and in the end Watt was simply beheaded after he had been hanged.

The process of the law here is of particular interest as they were charged under the process of Oyer and Terminer, an English legal procedure which did not have, nor ever has had, any standing in Scots law. This was because the Treason Act, passed in 1708 stated that anyone in the new United Kingdom charged with treason would be tried under English law.[5] This blatant disregard for the fact that the new country was formed from two independent nations both of which, according to the Treaty of Union would retain their own legal systems, is a perfect example of how Westminster has always seen Scotland since 1707. And the Scottish Justiciary were happy to go along with it. *Plus ça change.* The same process was used in the trials of the Strathaven weavers, Baird, Hardy and Wilson, after the abortive Rising of 1820, which was also set up by Government spies.

Sympathy for the ideas of the Radicals of the 1790s was widespread in Scotland and there is much more that awaits investigation. Things are improving in this area, though there are still those, particularly in the media, who are prone to make unfounded accusations of anti-English bias in such studies. Such accusations come from those addicted to supporting the prevailing Establishment line that emanates from the capital of England, from an Establishment whose attitudes can be fairly described as metrovincial, in that what is not of interest to them, they seem to truly believe, is of interest to no one. A better example of that than the Brexit vote, created by a playground spat between two grown men behaving like petulant adolescents would be hard to find.

That awareness of the problems inherent in the brutal expansion of the British Empire after Callender fled to America can be shown in the following. This is an excerpt from a remarkable piece of writing in Scots, *Bodkin's Proverbial Philosophy*, brought back to public attention in William Donaldson's grand book *The Language of the People* (1989). Its author is Tammas Bodkin, the pen-name of William Duncan Latto (1823-1899), the then editor of the 'People's Journal' which printed the following piece, and many similar. It, too, shows that the notion of the politically docile Scot is hardly matched by the evidence.

This vicious habit o cryin' murder withoot sufficient cause is not confined to individuals, but is equally rampant amang mankind in their corporate an national capacity. No tae gang far frae hame, I could point oot a nation that has of late had a lang spell at cryin' murder although it was patent to everybody wi' an unprejudiced ee that the complainant was the only pairty that showed ony disposition to shed bluid. Oor present rulers, wha hae been, in plain terms, a curse not only to this country, but to the haill warld for the by past five or sax years, hae been, if ye tak their word for't, sair, sair haudden doon by thae ruffians o' Afghans an Zulus, an' yet the curious thing is, they've aye managed to be uppermost. There was the late Shere Ali, for example, he was a most ootrageous tyke, it wad seem, wha was constantly plottin the ruin o' oor Indian Empire. Lord Lytton cried murder; oor rulers at hame re-echoed the cry; an' the result was that, although the Afghan ruler was doin' us nae harm whatsomever, he was huntit to death, an his son an successor robbit o a big slice o his dominations. I dinnae wonder a bit that the Khans has kickit up a row aboot the peace o Gandamak and murdered the members o' the Embassy. The victims are to be pitied, but them wha sent them to Cabul are sair tae blame. We had nae business to meddle wi the Afghans ava.

In light of recent history, this is remarkable.

1. http://www.stamp-shop.com/tytler/
2. https://archive.org/details/cihm_20802
3. Millar, A H 1923 *Haunted Dundee* Malcolm MacLeod Dundee p76ff
4. Meikle, HW 1912 *Scotland and the French Revolution* Maclehose Edinburgh p150 ff
5. https://en.wikipedia.org/wiki/Treason_Act_1708

A Scottish Patriot

I REMEMBER MY uncle Stewart who fought with the Gordon Highlanders throughout WWII saying that he had joined up to fight the Nazis, not to defend the British Empire. There were many Communists like him, and others, who saw a need to oppose Nazism but were none too happy to be in a British uniform. Others, however, saw things differently. Just as the figure of Winston Churchill on the one hand has tended to be politically beatified by the British establishment, so, on the other, facts around the levels of dissent during the years 1939-45 have very much been bypassed or ignored in most popular accounts. Although the Establishment storyline of the past seventy years has attempted to portray WWII as a simple war of good versus evil, more and more people in the world are aware that history can hardly be that simple, it is after all a story of the human past, and human beings are not simple creatures, and nor are their actions.

One man who stands out in this period in Scotland in particular, both for the arguments he put forward and for how he was treated by the so-called justice system, is Douglas Young, who was to be elected Chairman of the SNP in 1942. Like others who opposed the war Young has been vilified as a Nazi supporter yet he was nothing of the sort, unlike various members of the British Royal family and host of others amongst the so-called 'upper classes'. His case provides a salutary lesson in dealing with the entrenched power of the British State, still to this day lost in dreams of an Empire long gone, and thirled to the interests of the super-rich.

Douglas Young was a man of many talents: a poet, linguist, translator, scholar and political activist. By the late

1930s he was lecturing in Greek at Aberdeen University, and in 1938 he left the Labour Party to join the SNP. When Britain declared war in 1939 SNP policy was clear, if a bit unrealistic. The party opposed conscription unless it was to be controlled by a Scottish parliament. This from the British establishment position was tantamount to treason; after all it is emblazoned deep in the psyche of British politicians that democracy ends at the ballot box: gie's yer vote and dae's ye're tellt! There were many people who opposed the war and refused to fight, generally known as conscientious objectors, and the government was prepared to recognise that for religious and other reasons there would be people they could not force to try and kill other human beings. So they devised a scheme in which men refusing to fight could be conscripted to work down the mines, or in other industries deemed necessary to the war effort. Of course this would be helping to keep up the profits of those who owned such industries for whom this was not a time of sacrifice but an enhanced opportunity for profit. Have you ever heard of a capitalist government that asked the ultimate sacrifice of business – that they reduce their profit margins in time of war for the good of the nation?

The initial round of conscription had passed Young by because of his age, but with increasing casualties that some saw as a result of the general ineptitude and incompetence of the British High Command, the demand for more men arose and older men began to be conscripted. It came as no surprise to anyone when Young refused to go to war, but he *also* refused to register as a conscientious objector.

So it was that Douglas was called before Sheriff Sam Mac-Donald in Glasgow on April 13th, 1942, charged with ignoring his draft notice, despite the almost certainty that he would have been turned down for the draft because of his health. Drawing attention to how badly the war was going he said, 'To judge by recent results there is great doubt about the capacity of the British government to defend Scotland, which is my country. It is no service to Scotland to follow the misleadership of the British government and become a prisoner at St. Valery-en-Caux or at Singapore or elsewhere'. He went on to say that it was high time that the Scots fought for their own independence just as the Serbs and Norwegians were doing against the Nazis. This was too much for the Sherriff who ordered him to be silent. The SNP printed his entire speech including the section:

> Your Lordship will have noted the frequent observations made by war-minded publicists that the population of Scotland is apathetic or unduly complacent with regard to the present hostilities. This is principally due to the obvious fact that the Scots are not fighting for any Scottish cause; we do not enjoy national independence, nor is the liberty of Scotland among the war-aims or peace-projects of the British and allied governments...'

Young was prosecuted on the grounds that he was in breach of the National Service (Armed Forces) Act of 1941. He argued against this on several grounds: that the Act was against the Common Law of Scotland, which was protected by the Treaty of Union; that the Treaty of Union had not given the British Parliament the right to draft Scotsmen; that the so-called 'British' Parliament was in fact the English Parliament; and that Great Britain had voided the Treaty of Union and thus had no right to pass laws for Scotland. This latter point has surfaced over the past few decades again in regard to the Poll Tax, which was a clear breach of the Treaty of Union in that it enacted a law in Scotland that did not pertain to other parts of the United Kingdom. But entrenched power is rarely concerned with the niceties of law, unless it is to its advantage. The upshot of the trial was pretty much a foregone conclusion: the Sheriff, Sam MacDonald, congratulated Young on his scholarship and promptly sentenced him to 12 months' imprisonment. Bail was granted, and Young was temporarily set free to organize an appeal against the sentence. The SNP took advantage of the situation to vote him in as Chairman of its High Council, thus illustrating that Young's ideas and actions had some level of support in Scotland at the time.

His appeal was called for the 9 July, to be heard in the High Court by Lord Justice-General (Lord Normand), Lord Fleming and Lord Carmont. His argument was that the National Service in question was:

1. contrary to the Common Law of Scotland;
2. contrary to the Scoto-Anglic Treaty of Union which constituted the United Kingdom of Great Britain with the British Parliament;
3. unknown to the Law of Scotland, being that of a foreign state, *viz.* the Kingdom of England;
4. a fundamental nullity, being a pretended statute of what is no a legal non-entity, *viz.* the so-called Great Britain, which is deficient in the qualifications of a legal personality by International Law.

The three judges heard him out and then, rejecting his appeal, they ruled that his argument that 'All the acts of the Imperial Parliament since 1707 were void and of no effect' was invalid. The only problem was that Douglas Young had never put forward that proposition. It is not special pleading to point this out, as that is supposedly the raison d'etre of the judicial process: to address specific points of established statute law. Arguments must be specific to the matter in hand, and at no time had Young said that. It made no difference; the court had spoken on behalf of entrenched power and Young was wheeched back to prison where he was a common prisoner from 1 July 1942 to 10 March 1943. The members of the bench that day had clearly never heard the idea that justice must not just be done, but be seen to be done. There were many among the legal profession at that point who were uneasy about the behaviour of the judges.

And there were many outside the law trade who were likewise uneasy, to such an extent that Young was seen as something of a hero by a considerable number of Scots. In February

1944, he stood in a by-election for the seat of Kirkcaldy Burghs and despite a great deal of misrepresentation of his principles and behaviour (sound familiar?) garnered 6,621 votes, against the winning tally of the Government (Labour) candidate who polled 8,268. A month after this, a new prosecution was brought against Young, led by the Ministry of Labour, under the leadership of that great Socialist, Ernest Bevin. Young was now charged with contravening Regulation 80B of the Defence (General) Regulations 1939, for his personal non-compliance with the British industrial conscription. On 12 June, 1944, he was found guilty at Paisley Sheriff-Court and the Sheriff Substitute, AM Hamilton, added that the arguments put forward by the defence, which were all based on matters of constitutional law, were 'too lofty for this court', stating that they should properly be dealt with by a Supreme Court, such as that presided over by the Lord Justice-Clerk.

Young again appealed and got ready to present his arguments to the Judiciary Appeal Court. It is worth considering the details of what transpired in the High Court of Justiciary in Edinburgh on the 6 October 1944.

On the bench was the Lord Justice-Clerk (Lord Cooper), Lord Mackay, and Lord Stevenson. The quotes are from a pamphlet called *An Appeal to Scots Honour by Douglas Young* which was published in 1944 by the Scottish Secretariat. This is a verbatim report of what happened that day in court.

> **Lord Justice-Clerk:** Before the case I wish to say that I and my colleagues have received through the post within the past few days a printed document which I examined sufficiently to enable me to discover its character and find that it consists of a report with a commentary upon the proceedings which took place in this case at the Sheriff Court in Paisley on 12th June 1944. The document appears in my case to have been with the author's compliments. I wish to say with emphasis that the sending of a communication with regard to a pending appeal to the Judges who have to hear that appeal is a grossly

improper act according to the law of Scotland and could be dealt with as a grave Contempt of Court.

The second thing I wish to say, Mr. Young is this. In this appeal which is before us the defence put forward in the Court below is formulated in the *Stated Case, page 5, between letters C and D*. On July 9th, 1942, previous appeal at your instance, against the Procurator Fiscal of Glasgow, the same proposition was maintained before this court, then constituted of the Lord Justice-General, Lord Fleming and Lord Carmont. On that occasion the Lord Justice-General, giving the principal opinion, rejected that argument, with the concurrence of Lord Fleming and Lord Carmont, the argument being that, 'All of the Acts of the Imperial Parliament since 1707 were void and of no effect.' This is a binding decision on this Court. The proposition is no longer open to argument. I wish accordingly to ask you – Have you any other proposition to maintain to-day, and if so, what is it?

The Appellant: The proposition is that the Acts of the British Parliament instituted by the Treaty of Union, which are repugnant to that Treaty, are beyond the powers of that Parliament and accordingly are void.

Lord Justice-Clerk: That is the same proposition which was rejected in this court in 1942, and that proposition we are bound to reject. We are not prepared to hear further argument in favour of that argument. It would be a waste of judicial time. Have you any other proposition?

The Appellant: My Lords, the final proposition which I wish to lay before you your Lordships is this: that, even if your Lordships hold that the Emergency Powers Acts are valid, those Acts do not repeal Article XVIII of the Treaty of Union, and their general terms are not consistent with that Article. Accordingly, these Acts do not authorize the Ministry of Labour or his officers to ignore Article XVIII of the Treaty of Union in giving effect to Regulations made under these Acts. Article XVIII provides that 'no alteration can be made in laws which concern private right, except for evident utility of the subjects within Scotland.' There is therefore an onus on the Crown to prove that this invasion of my liberty was for the evident utility of the subjects within Scotland...

Lord Justice-Clerk (interrupting): That argument is simply an additional argument that the Acts of the Imperial Parliaments are *ultra vires*.

The Appellant: Yes, my Lords, that is my principle contention...

Lord Justice-Clerk (interrupting): The Appellant has been given two opportunities of indicating whether he has any other proposition to submit additional to that which was rejected by this Court in July 1942. In view of his failure to bring any other proposition forward the Court refuses to tolerate a repetition of the arguments directed to the proposition. I wish to move that the appeal be dismissed.

The Lord Justice-Clerk thereupon rose, turned his back, and resumed his seat. Lord Mackay and Lord Stevenson, without speaking arose, turned their backs, and resumed their seats.

Lord Justice-Clerk: Mr. Solicitor-General, do you wish a warrant for arrest? Call the next case.

And off went Douglas to prison in Edinburgh.

The note to which Cooper had referred was from the Sheriff Substitute in Paisley and said, 'The defence was that the Emergency Powers Act, 1939, under which the said Regulations were made, was *ultra vires* of the British Parliament and was of no force or effect in Scotland and that accordingly the said direction was inept.' *Ultra vires* means, beyond the competence. The prepared arguments had not been tested because that same Sheriff-Substitute had said, on the record, that they were too lofty for his court. And now they were not tested again. And the judgment in 1942 was given on a statement that Douglas Young had never made.

This is not the story that has been presented since, and such opposition to the war has been air-brushed out of our history.

The arguments which Douglas Young had compiled have never been heard in a Court of Law but can be found in the pamphlet, the full title of which is *An Appeal to Honour by Douglas Young: A Vindication of the Right of the Scottish People to FREEDOM from Industrial Conscription and Bureaucratic Despotism under the TREATY OF UNION with ENGLAND*, from which the verbatim report above is taken. Douglas later wrote:

> The question raised was, of course, that of federal constitutionalism, a question perfectly familiar to every American and Australian [...] It was not enough for a sheriff or other judge to take refuge behind an Act of the Westminster Parliament if that Parliament itself had its powers restricted by an Act of two Parliaments, namely the terms of union, an international treaty, between Scotland and England. The English have been accustoming themselves to the dogma of the omnipotence of Parliament, but such a dogma is untenable in relation to Scotland, whose Parliament was never omnipotent, and is incompatible with the Treaty of Union which constituted the British Parliament to begin with.

At the very least this is an argument that should have been heard and dealt with according to the law. But there's the rub – which law? The contention that the Westminster Parliament was acting beyond its powers surfaced again in the stramash over the introduction of the Poll Tax in Scotland in 1989, a year before it was brought in to England and Wales. Despite the widespread resistance to this pernicious legislation in Scotland it was the disturbances that it caused south of the border that saw its replacement by the Community Charge, which is just a watered-down version of the same thing, designed primarily to shift the burden of taxation from the well-off to those further down the economic scale.

There was discussion at that time of trying to raise the matter of a breach of the Treaty of Union, yet there was a Catch 22. At that point the Supreme Court had not been brought into being and the highest official court in the United Kingdom was the House of Lords. There had been a long-standing convention in that gravy train for superannuated politicians and business people who have donated to the various parties, that they would not rule on matters pertaining to Scots constitutional law. This meant that if there had been enough support for the idea of taking the case of a breach of the Treaty of Union of 1707 to any international tribunal, it would have failed at the first hurdle – it had not been through the entire legal process in the country of origin. The law as it stands is a bulwark of the State, not a control on it.

In Young's case his arguments were not heard, and during wartime the judges were perfectly aware that, though many people were uneasy at their actions, no one would do anything about it. Recently we have seen that it took 27 years to win official recognition of even the criminality at the heart of the Hillsborough disaster because of the entrenched defensiveness of State power, in that case effectively shielding the local police force. The contempt with which the bereaved people of Liverpool have been treated is particularly scunnersome, but it is one with the contempt that has been shown towards most places outside of the south east of England where power lies.

This is why history matters. We must not forget that we are members of a political union even if the Establishment at Westminster has treated Scotland as having been absorbed into England ever since the Treaty of Union. The complicity of those in Scotland who helped, and continue to help them, is quite clear in the behaviour of those judges at Douglas Young's appeal. The matters of law, the lessons of history were as nothing in the face of their duty – which was the continuing support of entrenched power at Westminster.

Young himself, being a true Scot did not behave as he might have been expected to in the years after the end of the WWII. Although he was a member of the SNP, joining the party in 1938, he had before that been a member of the Labour Party. We should not forget that the Labour Party, as founded by Keir Hardie, did not just advocate Home Rule for Scotland but also for all the colonies and dominions of the British Empire. Even though Young had in fact left the Labour Party, he still resigned from the SNP in 1948, after their new constitution placed a proscription on members being a member of any other political party. Even as leader of the SNP from 1942 on, he had argued for dual membership. Above all he was a man of principle, re-joining the Labour Party in June 1951, after becoming concerned at the slimness of their parliamentary majority after the 1950 general election.

Like many at the time he thought that the Scottish Covenant, a call for Home Rule signed by over two million Scots in that year, was a step on the road to independence:

> We, the people of Scotland who subscribe to this Engagement, declare our belief that reform in the constitution of our country is necessary to secure good government in accordance with our Scottish traditions and to promote the spiritual and economic welfare of our nation.

> We affirm that the desire for such reform is both deep and widespread through the whole community, transcending all political differences and sectional interests, and we undertake to continue united in purpose for its achievement.

> With that end in view we solemnly enter into this Covenant whereby we pledge ourselves, in all loyalty to the Crown and within the framework of the United Kingdom, to do everything in our power to secure for Scotland a Parliament with adequate legislative authority in Scottish affairs.

Despite repeated attempts, Young never managed to obtain a professorship in Scotland, moving to McMaster University in Canada as Professor of Greek in 1968 before moving to the University of North Carolina at Chapel Hill the following year. It seems he was not considered a suitable candidate for the various professorships he applied for in his native Scotland. A man of diverse talents and great energy, he was president of Scottish PEN from 1958 to 1962, and in 1967 he helped to found the 1320 Club, which looked to set up a nationalist alternative to the SNP. He died in America in 1973.

Postscript

THE QUESTION OF Scottish sovereignty is one of the aspects of our past that has cropped up regularly over the years, as anyone who looks at our history quickly learns. When Scotland and England came together through the 1707 Treaty of Union, the two Parliaments had different concepts of sovereignty. The Westminster Parliament, since 1688 and the bringing in of William of Orange to replace the House of Stewart, was working on the basis that Parliament itself was sovereign, through the legal entity known as the Crown in Parliament. This is the English doctrine of constitutional monarchy. Things in Scotland could hardly have been more different. Here the people were sovereign. This had been made clear as early as the 1320 Declaration of Arbroath, though there are grounds for thinking it developed even earlier and may be very old indeed. However, this was the basis for the various challenges to the power of the monarchy that arose in Scotland in the sixteenth and seventeenth centuries as delineated by my friend Donald Smith in our book Scotland's Democracy Trail.[1] The different concepts of sovereignty are not mentioned in the Treaty of Union, which was a contract between two distinct legal and constitutional entitles. The attitude of Westminster from the off, aided and abetted by the attitudes of the various monarchs involved, was that Westminster purportedly had absorbed the Scottish Parliament and that England had absorbed Scotland. This arrogant contempt for the realities of our separate histories has no legal basis in law and, as we have seen, as early as 1708 the Treason Act was passed stating that anyone being tried for treason in GB was to be tried under English law. This was a clear breach of the Treaty of Union but the placemen from Scotland murmured not. Likewise, there was then, and since, not a peep from the supposedly independent Scots law system. Effectively *force majeure* was the order of the day and Scotland was treated as if it had been subsumed into England, with the fig leaf of a separate law, church and education system. However, legal matters are not supposed to be subject to the whim of politicians.

The matter of Scottish sovereignty has raised its head several times since the Wanchancy Covenant. One particular case states matters very clearly. In 1953 John McCormick and Ian Hamilton raised a court case claiming that Elizabeth Windsor had no right to call herself Elizabeth II as there had been no previous Queen Elizabeth of the UK, or of Scotland.[2] Unsurprisingly their case was dismissed, despite the obvious truth of their claim. The British Government of course had form in this area, Lizzie's uncle having had his short reign in 1936 as Edward VIII. On appeal, it was ruled by three Scottish Law Lords that the Treaty of Union had no provision concerning the numbering of monarchs, so it was part of the royal prerogative to do what they liked in the matter. Then the Lord President, Lord Cooper made this statement, 'the principle of unlimited sovereignty of Parliament is a distinctively English principle and has no counterpart in Scottish constitutional law'. Established power at Westminster, as arrogant as ever, ignored this, as did the members of our oh-so-independent Scottish legal trade.

If Cooper was right, and the facts would tend to suggest he was, sovereignty only needs us to express it – but for too many Scots, thirled to the idea that their personal positions of status and wealth require the continuing existence of the British state, or even more sadly, still prepared to believe the blatant lies and distortions that emanate from the British Establishment and their poodles in the media, particularly the increasingly odious BBC, are still too feart to stand up for themselves. Most people are not overly fond of change and there is undoubtedly an entrenched small-c conservatism particularly amongst our older generation. That said, the young folk are moving in the direction of re-asserting our independence, so there is hope.

Over the years I have been regularly (too regularly?) making the point that the term Wars of Independence used to describe the struggles led by Wallace and Bruce against English invasion is a misnomer. It implies that Scotland had to win its independence from England and that is a lie. A deliberate and oft-repeated lie fostered by those who see their own advantage in continuing the Union. Also the on-going acceptance of too many of our politicians that we are beholden to the English for our Parliament is rooted in another lie. And that lie is that English Parliamentary sovereignty trumps the democratic aspirations of the Scottish people. We are one of two members of the original United Kingdom and it is our right, based on Scottish sovereignty to withdraw from that union and it does not require the assent of any English or British institution. What it does require is a generation of courageous Scottish politicians prepared to admit that the Westminster model of governance is not one that is of much use in our quest to remove the democratic deficit that has plagued us for three hundred and ten years, and counting.

As I write this, a story has appeared that illustrates the inherent corruption of public life on this island. It has been reported in the press that the Speyside Tulchan estate is for sale. As MSP Andy Wightman has pointed out, this is not actually true.[3] What is for sale is the shares in the company that owns the estate. This neatly gets round provisions in the new land legislation in Scotland which would have seen the tenant farmers of the estate having the right to purchase their farms. This use of law is not only clearly unjust, but directly flies in the face of the will of the Scottish Parliament. Similarly, it has recently become public knowledge that hundreds of Scotland's schools are in fact owned under PFI – the Profit First Initiative put in place by Labour in Scotland – by offshore investment funds.[4] That this sucks money from public funds to fill the coffers of the rich is the whole point of this appalling process, but according to the ex-leader of Edinburgh City Council, one Donald Anderson, speaking on a television news bulletin, it does not matter who owns the schools as long as they are well-run! This is an incredible statement, particularly in light of the recent scandal that saw seventeen such schools shut for emergency repairs, resulting in widespread disruption for pupils and their families. And with breathtaking duplicity the mainstream media have attempted to suggest that PFI is the fault of the current administration, totally ignoring the sleazy role of both Unionist Labour and Tories in creating this robbers' charter.

The reality of the British state is that the current administration, like their predecessors, are dedicated above all else to upholding the interests of the City of London, the world's capital of money-laundering, and as the Panama Papers showed, corruption sits at the very heart of British politics.

One of the slick tricks of the Westminster system has always been to make people think that their game is the only game in town, that the British parliamentary system is actually democratic and thus that matters political should be left to professional politicians. Well look where that has got us. In such a 'democracy' money blatantly buys influence, and the self-serving prosper.

The Brexit fiasco is a direct result of that system, but there are many severe disadvantages for the population at large and even the country itself that follow from the current system. Currently, attention is being drawn to the decrease in wildlife that has come about through the industrialization of agriculture. This process is always trumpeted in the mainstream media as a result of a drive for greater efficiency in food production. That is a lie. The process is simply driven by the lust for profit, as is the currently unfolding scandal of North Sea decommissioning. Our political parties are not set up to take on vested interests. Westminster style political parties are built to serve those interests - even in Scotland, where within our own parliament, the struggle to develop a sensible land policy is like walking through treacle. Politics is in fact far too important to be left to those looking to make a living from it and we must realise that true power lies, as the British system pretends to acknowledge but thwarts at every turn, with the people – with us. To that end I believe that we need to widen both the debate and political activity, and here's a thought – why not have fun doing it. Scotland's increasing politicisation has followed on a cultural revival that has been going on since the 1950s. So let us sing and dance, paint and sculpt, tweet and Instagram and generally have a bit of a laugh as we convince the doubters that the only safe future for our nation is to leave the Union and reassert our true national identity as a sovereign nation.

Luath Press Limited

committed to publishing well written books worth reading

LUATH PRESS takes its name from Robert Burns, whose little collie Luath (*Gael.*, swift or nimble) tripped up Jean Armour at a wedding and gave him the chance to speak to the woman who was to be his wife and the abiding love of his life. Burns called one of the 'Twa Dogs' Luath after Cuchullin's hunting dog in Ossian's *Fingal*.

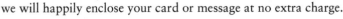

Luath Press was established in 1981 in the heart of Burns country, and is now based a few steps up the road from Burns' first lodgings on Edinburgh's Royal Mile. Luath offers you distinctive writing with a hint of unexpected pleasures.

Most bookshops in the UK, the US, Canada, Australia, New Zealand and parts of Europe, either carry our books in stock or can order them for you. To order direct from us, please send a £sterling cheque, postal order, international money order or your credit card details (number, address of cardholder and expiry date) to us at the address below. Please add post and packing as follows: UK – £1.00 per delivery address; overseas surface mail – £2.50 per delivery address; overseas airmail – £3.50 for the first book to each delivery address, plus £1.00 for each additional book by airmail to the same address. If your order is a gift, we will happily enclose your card or message at no extra charge.

Luath Press Limited
543/2 Castlehill
The Royal Mile
Edinburgh EH1 2ND
Scotland
Telephone: +44 (0)131 225 4326 (24 hours)
email: sales@luath. co.uk
Website: www. luath.co.uk